Corporate Acquisitions and Mergers in Italy

Corporate Acquisitions and Mergers in Italy

Guido Testa
Filippo Cristaldi
Orrick, Herrington & Sutcliffe LLP

This book was originally published as a chapter in Corporate Acquisitions and Mergers.

General Editor: Peter Begg

Wolters Kluwer

Published by:
Kluwer Law International B.V.
PO Box 316
2400 AH Alphen aan den Rijn
The Netherlands
E-mail: lrs-sales@wolterskluwer.com
Website: www.wolterskluwer.com/en/solutions/kluwerlawinternational

Sold and distributed by:
Wolters Kluwer Legal & Regulatory U.S.
7201 McKinney Circle
Frederick, MD 21704
United States of America
E-mail: customer.service@wolterskluwer.com

ISBN 978-94-035-0086-7

e-Book: ISBN 978-94-035-4875-3
web-PDF: ISBN 978-94-035-4885-2

Contents

Orrick, Herrington & Sutcliffe LLP

Orrick consistently ranks among a handful of global law firms with the breadth and calibre of practice to serve the complex needs of a discerning client base.

With more than twenty-five offices in Asia, Europe and North America, Orrick offers its clients a local understanding of business and the law combined with a global perspective.

Orrick opened its Milan office in 2003 and its Rome office in 2004. Today, Orrick has around 130 lawyers and several special counsels in Italy, all highly regarded individuals who rank among Italy's leading lawyers.

Our clients in Milan and Rome include many of the world's leading financial institutions, commercial enterprises, private equity funds and public companies.

Orrick's presence in Milan and Rome enhances the firm's ability to serve clients throughout Europe, including the other European financial and commercial centres of Düsseldorf, Munich, Brussels, London, Paris and Geneva. As in all our European offices we provide a blend of English, US and local legal capability. Moreover, our lawyers in Milan and Rome have direct access to Orrick's extensive legal, technological and other professional resources.

Lawyers in our Milan and Rome offices offer the following cross-border and domestic legal services:

Corporate Transactions, M&A and Private Equity	Intellectual Property and Data Protection
Banking and Capital Markets	Litigation
Debt Restructuring and Bankruptcy	Administrative Law and Real Estate
Compliance Programmes Related to Criminal Liabilities of Companies and Financial Crimes	Energy and Project Finance Tax Finance
Competition Law	
Employment Law	
Market Regulation	

Address:

Orrick, Herrington & Sutcliffe
Corso Matteotti 10
20121 Milano

Italy
Tel.: +39 0245413800
Fax: +39 0245413801
E-mail: gtesta@orrick.com
fcristaldi@orrick.com

1 INTRODUCTION

[01] Italy is an important force in the European Union (EU), being one of the founding members and one of the four major vote holders. With its strong economic performance in commerce and industry, Italy has proved no exception to the list of countries which have experienced, in recent years, a surge in the number of mergers and acquisitions of businesses. Italy is an important player in the European M&A scenario.

[02] For the foreign investor, Italy offers favourable fiscal, company and banking legislation and practices. There are no legal restrictions or limitations on foreign participation in Italian companies, partnerships or joint ventures, nor on the establishment of branch offices or subsidiaries. With the comprehensive changes in exchange control regulations which came into effect in January 1989, Italy has come into line with generally adopted principles whereby (with the exception of a small number of specific limitations) all the normal international currency transactions are permitted. In substance, there are virtually no restrictions on the transfer of currency between residents and non-residents. In particular, no restrictions apply to the payment abroad of dividends, interest and royalties, nor to the holding of foreign currencies in bank accounts, nor to the repatriation of the capital originally invested in Italy. Moreover, the banking system has developed significantly over the last few years. New laws, particularly those relating to the removal of monetary restrictions, and the reaction of the banks in the face of the onset of international competition, have combined to produce a wider range of better services.

[03] On the first examination, it is surprising to an observer from abroad how limited a role is played in the economy by the public, either directly or through the various stock exchanges (*la Borsa*). For instance, as of December 2021, there were only around 407 companies which enjoyed listed status. Moreover, a noticeable characteristic of shares which are publicly traded in Italy is that they generally represent only a minor interest in the company concerned. Hence, they are usually of little significance in terms of corporate power. The securities system for raising funds in the public markets is relatively underdeveloped and, while the people of Italy are noted for the amount of savings made in relation to earnings, they are equally noted for reinvesting a comparatively small proportion of these savings into the Italian financial markets. Most of the finance required for investment is procured from various sources of credit rather than looking to the equity markets. By British and American standards, an atypical amount of commerce and industry in Italy is privately and closely controlled by groups and families.

[04] Another noticeable trait restricting the free market for control of the business in Italy is the high degree of influence exercised by the State, directly or indirectly, in the commercial and industrial sectors. Moreover, where the State has a direct or indirect controlling interest in a company, the relevant ministry frequently reserves for itself the ultimate right, within its own discretion, to authorize any merger or sale. The Italian legislature issued Law Decree No. 386 of 5 December 1991, by which provisional and procedural grounds were established for improved organization of businesses owned by the State through their transformation into joint-stock companies. Placing of such shares has been effected in compliance with criteria established by the Ministry of the Treasury, with a view to ensuring the maintenance of control over such enterprises by the State. In addition, this Decree also provided for progressive privatization of some assets and businesses owned by the State.

[05] The leaders of industry, commerce and government recognize, however, the generally accepted need for corporate reconstruction and development in order to meet the challenges and opportunities offered by advances in technology and the opening of the Single Market. This explains both the perceptible increase in the number and rate of mergers and acquisitions and the fact that they have almost invariably been agreed upon as off-market transactions. Hostile takeovers, in such a closed and tightly controlled economy, have little chance of playing such a large role in Italy as they do in the United States (US) or the United Kingdom (UK). It is possible that the climate for such transactions may be becoming more favourable. Observers of the economy have argued that a trend is gradually developing toward increased participation by private investors in stock ownership.

2 LOCAL ECONOMIC AND POLITICAL ASPECTS

[06] Italy is located on the southern side of Europe and due to its geographical position represents a bridge, both from a commercial and cultural point of view, between Central Europe, on one side, and the Northern African and Middle East Countries, on the other side. With a surface area of 301 340 square kilometres and a population of around 59.2 million, Italy is one of the main European Countries. The growth of the Italian population is quite stable, as the birth rate is equal to around 0.3% per year.

2.1 Economic Aspects

[07] From an economic standpoint, Italy has a market-oriented economy, which is characterized by a huge number of small and medium-sized firms, with a wide and varied industrial basis.

[08] Since the end of World War II, Italy has experienced a strong change in its economy, which has transformed a hitherto underdeveloped country (at the beginning of the 1950 more than 40% of the population was employed in the agricultural sector), into one of the most powerful economies in the World. That happened as a consequence of a period of continued economic growth, which lasted until the end of the twentieth century. However, from the beginning of the present century, this process has slowed down, and Italy has experienced a phase of stabilization and reduced growth. The growth period was at its peak in the years between 1950 and 1970 (the so-called *economic boom period*). During this period, Italy experienced a progressive reduction in the importance of the primary sector (represented by agriculture, breeding and fishery) in favour of the development of the manufacturing industry and the service industry. From a social point of view, this process has been accompanied by deep transformations in the productive infrastructure, with a huge immigration process from the regions of southern Italy to the more industrialized regions of the north-west of the country.

[09] Currently, the Italian economy remains one of the most important in the World. On the basis of data supplied by the International Monetary Fund (2018–2019), the Italian economy is the eighth in the World in terms of nominal Gross Domestic Product (GDP) and the twelfth in terms of purchasing power, and as of today, it has become a model for sustainable growth. As we know, the year 2020, marked by the COVID-19 pandemic, has put a strain on the world's major economies, which have seen a portion of their wealth go up in smoke due to restrictions put in place to limit contagions. However, the National Institute of Statistics ('*Istituto Nazionale di Statistica*') specifies that in 2021 the Italian economy recorded growth of exceptional intensity due to the strong recovery of productive activity. GDP growth was driven above all by domestic demand, while foreign demand and the change in stocks made very limited contributions.

[10] Furthermore, Italy is a country strongly oriented towards foreign trade, ranking eighth in the World for export volumes and tenth in the World for import volumes. At the end of the last decade, Italian exports represented around 8% of the export flows within the EU, and more than 11% of the volumes of the export flows from the EU to the rest of the World. Exports represent around 30% of Italy's GDP, of which the principal destination countries are Germany, France, Spain, USA and the UK. Imports represent around 26.5% of Italy's GDP, and the main countries of origin of the imported products are Germany, France, China, the Netherlands, Libya and Russia (the products imported from these last two countries are represented mostly by oil and natural gas). Indeed, Italy's mineral resources (located primarily in southern Italy, in the Po valley and in the Adriatic Sea) are insufficient, and natural resources have to be imported from abroad.

[11] On the basis of data supplied by the Italian Trade & Investment Agency, the pandemic hit the Italian socio-economic fabric hard and led to a drop in exports which, however, was less than that recorded by other major exporting countries. Indeed, among the G8 countries, Italy is the second in terms of the smallest drop in exports and has performed much better than France, UK and US. The year 2021 began positively and brought our country's exports to results above pre-COVID levels. The customs value of Italy's exports of goods and services in 2020 was EUR509 billion and accounted for 29.5% of the country's GDP. Finally, Italy's market share of world exports of goods in 2020 (2.85%) remained stable compared to the previous year. The pandemic has acted as a catalyst for trends that were already underway, for society and, above all, for the productive world, which is now faced with the so-called 'twin transitions': the digital and ecological one. These changes will not distort 'Made in Italy', but will enhance its distinctive features: attention to quality, the environment and the human dimension will be crucial in laying the foundations for a more sustainable, inclusive and resilient recovery. The ability to combine innovation and creativity with respect for tradition and territory will therefore remain an essential factor for Italy's success in the post-pandemic world.

The Ministry of Foreign Affairs and International Cooperation is committed to accompanying companies in these processes and, thanks to the reform, which since last year has assigned to it the competences of defining the strategies of commercial and promotional policy with foreign countries and the development of internationalization, will continue to support the country and its economic fabric.

[12] As already observed, Italian industry is dominated by small and medium-sized firms, mostly manufacturing firms, while the number of large companies is relatively low in comparison with countries comparable to Italy in terms of population and size.

[13] The industrial sector represents around 30% of GDP, and the main industrial sectors are motoring (cars, motorcycles, spare parts and accessories), shipbuilding, rubber, metallurgy, pharmaceutical, energy, defence and agro-industrial. The main industrial production areas are located in the north of the country and, in particular, in Lombardy, Piedmont, Veneto and Emilia-Romagna.

[14] The most important sector of the Italian economy is the service industry, both in terms of the number of employees (around 67% of the total) and contribution to GDP (over 70%). Moreover, this sector is also the most dynamic, as it contains 70% of all new enterprises. The main activities linked to the service industries are tourism, commerce, personal services, banking and insurance.

[15] Lastly, it should be noted that since the end of the twentieth century, Italy has started to introduce new laws to deregulate the labour market and introduce more flexibility, also with the aim of encouraging foreign investment in the country.

[16] The economic downturn of the last few years in Europe has also impacted the M&A scene in Italy, with a consequent reduction in the number and size of transactions. However, there are signs of recovery in this sector which allow a more positive expectation for the future, also taking account of the first signs of a general economic recovery in Europe. The year 2021 was a record year for M&A activity with no less than 1 165 transactions carried out in Italy for a countervalue of around EUR98 billion from EUR44 billion in 2020 and EUR52 billion in 2019: this is the best figure since the 2008 financial crisis in terms of countervalue and the absolute record in terms of volume. With regard to the private equity market according to figures communicated by AIFI (the Italian private equity and venture capital association), in the first six months of 2021, there was a boom in the amount of money invested in both the private equity and venture capital sectors, which reached a record amount of EUR4 549 million.

2.2 Political Aspects

[17] Italy is a democratic republic and is organized as a civil law legal system. The Italian legal system, as set forth in the Constitution adopted in 1948, is based on the traditional principle of the division of the powers between (i) the executive power (represented by the government, headed by the Prime Minister), (ii) the legislative power (represented by the House of Parliament, which is divided into two houses of equal importance: the Chamber of Deputies and the Senate of the Republic), and (iii) the judiciary power. The President of the Republic is required to represent the nation, to guarantee compliance with the Constitution and to ensure the correct balance between these three powers. The territory of the Italian Republic is divided into twenty regions, which have certain legislative as well as administrative powers. Five regions (Valle d'Aosta, Trentino Alto Adige, Friuli Venezia Giulia, Sicily and Sardinia) enjoy an increased autonomy status.

3 REGULATORY FRAMEWORK

3.1 Corporate Structures

[18] The Italian corporate legal framework was thoroughly reformed pursuant to Legislative Decree No. 6 of 19 January 2003. In accordance with this regulation (and subsequent amendments thereto), the legal structures for carrying out commercial or industrial operations in Italy are essentially divided into corporations and partnerships, where the same basic distinctions as to liability are to be found as occur in England. In the case of corporations, or limited liability companies, the shareholders are generally liable only for the capital they have agreed to contribute to the corporation and no more.

With a partnership, on the other hand, liability is joint and generally unlimited and, therefore, may exceed the capital agreed to be invested in the venture. The legislator, with the introduction of the Decree Law of 24 April 2017 n. 50 (Corrective Decree), has rewritten the regulation of limited liability companies, granting them a series of opportunities, previously reserved to S.p.A.s (*Società per Azioni*, i.e., joint-stock companies). Such new opportunities are mainly related to the financing of the company as well as the circulation of interests in the corporate capital. Furthermore, Law No. 155/2017 has charged the Government to adopt new legislation to reform the law on insolvency and replace the 1942 Insolvency Law. Legislative Decree No. 14/2019 (called the 'Code of Corporate Crisis and Insolvency') introduced significant changes to the current insolvency discipline and to the corporate law as well, including:

(i) a new general principle for the management of companies, providing that companies have a duty to establish an organizational, administrative and accounting structure appropriate to the nature and size of the company, and to take steps without delay to implement one of the tools provided by law for overcoming the crisis and recovering company continuity;
(ii) a new discipline related to directors' liability, in cases of bankruptcy, and
(iii) new rules on the obligation to establish a controlling body in limited liability companies 'S.r.l.s' (*Società a responsabilità limitata* in Italian), the details of which are referred to in the section 3.7 'Controlling Body' below.

3.2 The Two Main Forms of Company: The *Società per Azioni* (S.p.A.) and the *Società a Responsabilità Limitata* (S.r.l.)

[19] Commercial and industrial entrepreneurs usually choose to incorporate corporations due to the benefits of limited liability. Of these, the most frequently used, and the most relevant from an economic viewpoint is the *Società per Azioni* (S.p.A.), often called the joint-stock company. This bears strong similarities to the English public limited company. It may be contrasted with the *Società a Responsabilità Limitata* (S.r.l.), often called the limited liability company, which, in turn, possesses certain similarities with the English private company.

[20] While in the past most of the rules governing the S.p.A. were also applicable to the S.r.l., with effect from January 2004, limited liability companies, because of the increased statutory relevance of the shareholders' personal participation in the company, have been regulated in accordance with different provisions. The legal structure is similar to a limited liability partnership: the S.r.l. is intended to meet the business needs of small and medium-sized firms, whose shareholders are directly involved in the management of the company. In view of the above, measures to protect investors are not necessary and freedom to govern the company is limited only by the need to protect possible claimants and third-party interests.

3.3 Corporate Capital

[21] The main differences between the S.p.A. and the S.r.l. lie in their minimum capital requirements and the marketability of their shares.

[22] As far as the minimum capital of the S.p.A is concerned, Decree Law No. 91 of 24 June 2014 modified the minimum threshold from EUR120 000.00 to EUR50 000.00. In an S.r.l., on the other hand, the minimum capital must be no less than EUR10 000.00, with the possibility of reducing this threshold to EUR1.00 under certain conditions determined by the law.

[23] The quotas of an S.r.l., unlike the shares of an S.p.A., may not be traded on the stock market.

[24] For both types of company, at least 25% of the corporate capital must be paid up upon incorporation, save in cases where there is a sole shareholder, in which case the corporate capital must be fully paid up. The holding of shares for the S.p.A. and quotas for the S.r.l. is generally nominative.

3.4 Incorporation

[25] As regards S.p.As, according to sections 2328, 2329 and 2330 of the Italian Civil Code, incorporation consists of a two-step process: (1) the execution of a public deed before a notary public, who is responsible for verifying compliance with the formal compulsory conditions required by law in order to incorporate the company; and (2) the filing of such public deed in the Companies' Register.

[26] The corporation does not come into existence until the deed of incorporation has been filed and duly registered in the Companies' Register.

[27] The deed of incorporation must set out, *inter alia*, the corporate name, the name of the city council where the registered office of the company is located, the purpose or objects of the corporation, the corporate capital, the number of shares and their par value, if any, the names of the directors and (by contrast with common law jurisdictions) the duration of the corporation (unless the company is incorporated for an unlimited period of time, in which case the deed of incorporation must indicate the notice period for any shareholders wishing to withdraw from the company). The internal management of the company is regulated by the law and its by-laws, and its objects are limited to those set out in the deed of incorporation. The objects clause, as well as any other clause of the by-laws, may be altered by resolution of the shareholders. The company must keep proper records, including, *inter alia*, a minute book of directors' and shareholders' meetings and its accounts. According to sections 2215*bis* of the Italian Civil Code, inserted by Law Decree No. 185 of 29 November 2008 (as implemented by Law No. 2 of 28 January 2009 and as amended by Law Decree No. 70 of 13 May 2011), such records may also be kept in electronic form.

[28] Dividends may not be paid out of capital but only out of income; nor may they be distributed before losses carried forward have been recouped. If, as a result of losses, the corporate capital is impaired by more than one-third, the directors are obliged by law to take certain formal steps including, if necessary, calling for a reduction of capital by the shareholders' meeting. If by reason of any losses, the capital falls below the minimum required by law, then the capital must be replenished, or the company reorganized, for example, by alteration from an S.p.A. to an S.r.l.

[29] One of the major novelties of the company law reform is that the deed of incorporation may be executed by a sole entity or by two or more entities (in each case, either a corporate entity or an individual person). In the event that the deed of incorporation has been executed by a sole entity, that entity is liable in respect of any obligations and claims incurred subject to the limit of the outstanding corporate capital only if: (i) the corporate capital of the company has been fully paid up; and (ii) a special declaration, stating that all the shares are held by a sole entity, has been duly filed in the relevant Companies' Register. In the absence of these two conditions, the sole shareholder bears unlimited liability. These two conditions must also be met during the life of the company if all the shares are held by a sole entity which is unwilling to assume full liability for obligations and claims which may be faced by the company. The shareholders may use a power of attorney for the purpose of the incorporation.

[30] According to Italian law, it is possible for S.p.A.s to issue special categories of shares, which grant their owners particular rights. In relation to non-listed companies, the following special categories of shares are regulated by the Italian Civil Code. In relation to voting rights, companies may issue: (i) non-voting shares; (ii) shares with voting rights limited to particular matters; (iii) shares with voting rights subject to the verification of non-merely 'potestative' conditions (i.e., conditions which depend on the arbitrary and exclusive will of one of the parties). Shares of this kind must not exceed half of the corporate capital, in order to avoid an excessive concentration of control of the company in the hands of those shareholders having full voting rights. The Italian Legislator has recently introduced the possibility of issuing 'shares with multiple votes', which grant their owner more than one vote (up to a maximum of three votes per share). Also, this kind of share may grant voting rights limited to special matters or subordinated to the verification of non-merely potestative conditions. Moreover, with regard to shares owned by the same shareholder, the by-laws of a company may provide that the voting rights: (i) shall be limited to a maximum extent; (ii) shall be staggered (e.g., one vote for each share up to 10% of the corporate capital; one vote for every two shares over 10% and up to 20% of the corporate capital, and so on).

[31] With reference to the right to share in profits, Italian law provides for a particular kind of share – called a 'privileged share' – which grants its owner a preferential right relating to (i) the sharing of profits; and/or (ii) reimbursement of capital on dissolution of the company. The company is free to regulate the economic aspects of such shares, subject only to the constraints of the so-called leonine pact, according to which, pursuant to section 2265 of the Italian Civil Code, any agreement which has the effect of totally excluding one or more shareholders from participating in a company's profit or liabilities is null and void. Under Italian Law, it is also possible to issue shares – called 'related shares' – whose economic rights (e.g., to distributions) are related to the results of the company's activities in a specific field of business. Other special categories of shares are those that may be freely offered by companies to particular employees. With reference to shares of this kind, companies can establish (i) specific rules relating to the form of the same; (ii) the manner of transfer; as well as (iii) relevant rights granted to the respective owners. Companies may also grant their employees financial instruments which are not shares and which, consequently, are not part of the corporate capital; being the owner of such an instrument does not confer the legal status of a shareholder. Such financial instruments may grant economic and administrative rights to their owners, but without conferring voting rights at general meetings of the shareholders.

3.5 Shareholders' Meetings

[32] As far as shareholders' meetings are concerned, a distinction may be made between ordinary and extraordinary shareholders' meetings. The major difference between these two kinds of meetings is based on the subject matter to be resolved, on the different majorities required in order to adopt the relevant resolutions, and on the different ways of drafting the relevant minutes (e.g., the minutes of an extraordinary shareholders' meeting must be drawn up by a public notary).

[33] According to section 2364 of the Italian Civil Code, the ordinary shareholders' meeting resolves upon: (i) the approval of the annual financial statements; (ii) the appointment and removal of the directors; (iii) the appointment of the statutory auditors and, if applicable, of the third-party auditors; (iv) the determination of the remuneration of the directors and of the statutory auditors, (if not determined in advance in the by-laws of the company); (v) the bringing of actions for liability against the directors and the statutory auditors; (vi) any other matter which may be submitted to it for resolution by law, as well as authorizations required under the by-laws relating to activities carried on by directors; and (vii) approval of the rules for conducting the shareholders' meeting if any.

[34] On the other hand, according to section 2365 of the Italian Civil Code, the extraordinary shareholders' meeting resolves upon: (i) amendments to the by-laws of the company; (ii) the appointment, substitution and powers to be granted to the liquidators; and (iii) any other matters submitted to its decision by the law.

[35] Pursuant to section 2368 of the Italian Civil Code, the first call ordinary shareholders' meeting is duly convened by the attendance of members representing not less than one-half of the company's capital, excluding from this computation any shares without voting rights. The meeting passes the resolution by an absolute majority unless a higher majority is required by the company's by-law. The first call extraordinary shareholders' meeting is duly convened and passes resolutions by an affirmative vote of members representing more than one-half of the capital of the company. Section 2369 of the Italian Civil Code provides for the possibility of second or further calls of the ordinary and extraordinary shareholders' meetings in the event that the resolution has not been adopted in the first call.

[36] The notices of shareholders' meetings of non-listed companies must be published fifteen days in advance in the Official Gazette of the Italian Republic. Moreover, the by-laws of non-listed companies may entitle the directors to call the shareholders' meeting by means of a notice sent to the shareholders (in such a manner as to assure proper evidence that each shareholder has obtained it) at least eight days before the shareholders' meeting. Moreover, the by-laws of the company may provide that the shareholders' meeting be held by means of telecommunications. In the absence of these formalities, the shareholders' meeting is deemed to be regularly constituted only when the entire corporate capital is represented and when a majority of the statutory auditors and of the directors attend the meeting.

[37] Notices of shareholders' meetings of listed companies must be published thirty days in advance on the company's website and by other means established by regulation by National Commission for Companies and the Stock Exchange (CONSOB), including publication in extract form in the daily newspapers.

[38] If the by-laws of the company so require, the shares must be physically deposited with the company's registered office or with the banks indicated in the notice, within the period set out in the by-laws. If the registered office is in Italy, both shareholders' and board meetings should generally be held in Italy unless the by-laws provide otherwise.

[39] As far as the S.r.l. is concerned, the quota holders resolve the issues indicated in the by-laws and matters that directors (or a specified number of the same quota holders representing one-third or more of the corporate capital) submit fo approval to the quota holders' meeting. The quota holders, in any event, have to

(1) approve the annual accounts and the distribution of profits;
(2) appoint, if provided by the by-laws, the directors of the company;
(3) appoint, in the cases stated under section 2477, the statutory auditors, the chairman of the board of auditors, or the third-party auditor;
(4) amend the by-laws;
(5) carry out transactions involving relevant changes to the core business of the company as provided in the by-laws or which cause serious restrictions to shareholders' rights.

[40] The by-laws may allow decisions to be adopted by 'written consultation' on the basis of a written proposal circulated among quota holders at the initiative of one of them, or by 'written consent' to a proposal not solicited by other quota holders (sec tion 2479 of the Italian Civil Code).

[41] Each quota holder is entitled to attend the quota holders' meeting and to vote in proportion to his participation in the corporate capital.

[42] If not differently provided for in the by-laws:

- the quota holders' meeting has to be called by registered letter mailed to each quota holder, at the address shown in the relevant Companies' Register at least eight days before the meeting;
- the quota holders may attend the meeting by proxy. The proxy has to be con ferred in writing, and the related documents must be kept by the company;
- a regular meeting is duly constituted with the presence of quota holders rep resenting at least one-half of the company's capital. The meeting adopt resolutions by an absolute majority;
- in the absence of a formal notice of call, a resolution is deemed to be regu larly adopted when the entire capital of the company is present or repre sented, and all the directors and members of the board of auditors are present or informed, and they do not oppose discussion of the relevant mat ters.

[43] A resolution of the quota holders' meeting which is not adopted in conformity with the law or the by-laws may be challenged by: (a) the quota holders that have not consented to such resolution; (b) the directors; and (c) the auditors, within three months from the date of filing in the book of quota holders' meetings (sec tions 2479ter of the Italian Civil Code).

3.6 Management

[44] One of the major innovations of the new company law framework relates to the structure and the different roles and/or functions pertaining to the various corporate bodies of the S.p.A. One of the major differences from the past is that the shareholders' meeting does not have a significant and general role in the management of the company; the shareholders' meeting can only resolve upon the few specific matters that are expressly and exclusively reserved to it by the law.

[45] On the other hand, the management body of the company is responsible for carrying out all business activities of the company which are not explicitly reserved to the shareholders' meeting or to the controlling body (i.e., the board of statutory auditors).

[46] The corporate law reform has provided new opportunities for selecting various sets of corporate governance rules that might prove to be appropriate for dealing with the management and control of the company, namely: the traditional system ('sistema tradizionale'), the two-tier system ('sistema dualistico') and the one-tier system ('sistema monistico').

[47] The traditional system is composed of the shareholders' meeting, the board of directors/sole director, the board of statutory auditors and, possibly (depending on the size of the company), the third-party auditors.

[48] The two-tier system is characterized by the interposition of an intermediate corporate body called the board of supervision ('consiglio di sorveglianza') between the shareholders' meeting and the company's board of management ('consiglio di gestione'). The management of the company is exclusively vested in the board of management, which is appointed by the board of supervision. This latter body is appointed by the shareholders' meeting and takes upon itself some of the functions which, under the traditional system, usually pertain to the shareholders' meeting (e.g., appointment and revocation of the board of management, approval of the financial statements, actions against members of the board of management) and to the statutory auditors (e.g., supervision of compliance with the law, the by-laws of the company and the principles concerning the correct management of the company).

[49] The one-tier system is characterized by the presence of a single corporate entity charged both with the management and the control of the company. A committee for the control of the management of the company ('comitato per il controllo sulla gestione') is appointed by and among the members of the board of directors and is aimed to fulfil the roles and functions of the statutory auditors.

[50] As regards the nationality of the directors, as a general rule a non-Italian citizen may hold the office of the director of an Italian company (theoretically, unless the company's by-laws provide otherwise, all the directors of a company may be non-Italian citizens). Under this profile, a non-Italian citizen may hold the office of the director of an Italian company (i) if he is a citizen of a country in the EU, or (ii) in the case of a non-EU citizen, if he is regularly residing in Italy (pursuant to section 2 paragraph 2, of Law No. 286/1998), or (iii) in the case of a non-EU citizen not residing in Italy, on the basis of reciprocity of conditions, i.e., if an Italian citizen would be entitled to hold the office of the director of a company of the country of which the individual in question is a citizen. In any case, a non-Italian director (and, in particular, those having management tasks) should ask for an Italian tax code.

[51] As far as the management of the company is concerned, it is necessary to distinguish between the traditional system ('sistema tradizionale'), the two-tier system ('sistema dualistico') and the one-tier system ('sistema monistico').

[52] In the traditional system, the company is managed by its directors (or by a sole director). In the event that the management is entrusted to more than one person, such persons constitute the board of directors. Pursuant to section 2381 of the Italian Civil Code, the board of directors may entrust some of its functions to a particular executive committee ('comitato esecutivo') formed by some of its members, or to one or more managing directors ('amministratore delegato').

[53] According to section 2383 of the Italian Civil Code, the directors are appointed by the ordinary shareholders' meeting for a period of time not exceeding three fiscal years and their tenure expires on the date of the shareholders' meeting convened for the approval of the financial statements related to the last fiscal year of their office. The termination of the directors' office by the expiration of their term is effective from the time when the board of directors has been reconstituted. Directors can be re-elected and can be removed by the shareholders' meeting at any time, even if they have been appointed in the company's by-laws, subject always to the director's right to compensation for damages if the removal occurs without cause.

[54] Pursuant to section 2385 of the Italian Civil Code, a director who resigns/renounces his office must give written notice to the board of directors and to the chairman of the board of statutory auditors. The renunciation is immediately effective if the majority of the board of directors remains in office or, if such is not the case, from the time when the majority of the board of directors has been reconstituted as a result of the acceptance of new directors.

[55] Pursuant to section 2386 of the Italian Civil Code, if, during the fiscal year, a vacancy of one or more directors occurs, the other directors provide for their replacement by resolution approved by the board of statutory auditors; if vacancies of the majority of the directors occur, those who remain in office have to call a shareholders' meeting to provide for the filling of the vacancies.

[56] The company's by-laws may contain provisions by which, should a vacancy of one or more directors occur, the entire board of directors is considered to have ceased ('simul stabunt, simul cadent').

[57] The presence of a majority of the directors in the office is necessary for the validity of resolutions of the board of directors unless the by-laws require a larger attendance (section 2388 of the Italian Civil Code).

[58] Resolutions of the board of directors are passed by an absolute majority unless the by-laws provide otherwise. Votes cannot be cast by proxy.

[59] The by-laws of the company may provide that the meeting of the board of directors be held by means of telecommunications.

[60] The fees and any share of the profits belonging to members of the board of directors and of the executive committee are provided for in the by-laws or, alternatively, are decided by the shareholders' meeting.

[61] Section 2391 of the Italian Civil Code states that a director must notify the other directors and the statutory auditors of any interest that he/she has, either on his/her own account or on behalf of third parties, with regard to any particular transaction of the company. The director in question must specify the nature, the terms, the origin and the relevance of such interest, and in the event he/she is the managing director, must refrain from carrying out the transaction.

[62] In the relevant resolution of the board of directors, all the reasons and the possible profits for the company that may derive from undertaking the relevant transaction must be explained in detail. If these provisions are not complied with, a resolution of the board of directors which has been adopted with the decisive vote of the director in conflict may be challenged if it is proved that such resolution has caused damage to the company. Any directors who acted in conflict of interest will be liable for the damages derived to the company as a result of their behaviour.

[63] The directors must fulfil their obligations as imposed on them by corporate law regulations and pursuant to the by-laws with due care and in accordance with their allotted role and their specific duties.

[64] The directors are jointly liable to the company for any damages deriving from the non-fulfilment of their duties, except for undertakings vested solely in the executive committee or in one or more of the directors. Actions for liability of the directors concerned may be pursued by the company subject to a resolution of the shareholders' meeting (that, if passed with the votes of at least 20% of the corporate capital, automatically implies the revocation of the director/s concerned). Actions for liability of the directors concerned may also be carried out by shareholders representing at least 20% of the company's corporate capital or such other percentage as may be determined by the by-laws, which percentage cannot, however, exceed one-third of the amount of the outstanding share capital.

[65] The directors are liable to the company's creditors for non-compliance with their duties concerning the preservation of the company's patrimonial assets, bearing in mind that the relevant legal action may be carried out only when the company's assets are insufficient for the fulfilment of creditors' monetary claims.

[66] In the two-tier system ('sistema dualistico'), the management of the company is carried out exclusively by the board of management, which undertakes all activities within the scope of the company's objects. The board of management may entrust a number of its tasks and duties to some of its members. Almost all the rules described above with regard to directors' discipline under the traditional system apply to the board of management as neatly established pursuant to section 2409*undecies* of the Italian Civil Code.

[67] In the one-tier system, the management of the company is carried out by the board of directors and by a committee comprising directors appointed by that board of directors ('comitato per il controllo sulla gestione'). Almost all the rules described above with regard to directors' discipline under the traditional system apply.

[68] With respect to the management of the S.r.l., unless otherwise provided in the by-laws, the management of the company has to be entrusted to one or more of its members appointed by the shareholders (in the case of S.r.l.s, the adoption of the two-tier system or of the one-tier system is not allowed). The company's directors may act jointly or separately according to the provisions set out in the by-laws and pursuant to the rules stated in sections 2257 and 2258 of the Italian Civil Code.

[69] All the directors of an S.r.l. have a general power to represent the company (i.e., notwithstanding any provision to the contrary that may be contained in the by-laws). Limitations on the power of representation set out in the by-laws, even if published, are not binding on third parties, unless it is proved that the latter acted wilfully to the detriment of the company (sections 2475*bis* of the Italian Civil Code).

[70] Any agreements entered by directors having a conflict of interest with the company may be cancelled at the request of the company, whenever the conflict was known by the counterparty.

[71] Resolutions of the board of directors, adopted by means of the vote of a director who has an interest in conflict with that of the company, and which cause injury to the company, may, within three months from the relevant date, be attacked by the directors and, if appointed, by the persons indicated under section 2477 of the Italian Civil Code.

[72] In all cases, rights acquired in good faith by third parties on the basis of acts performed in the implementation of the resolution are unaffected (sections 2475*ter* of the Italian Civil Code).

[73] The directors are jointly liable (in solido) to the company for damages deriving from duties in relation to the management of the company, which are imposed upon them by the law and by the by-laws. However, liability for acts or omissions of directors does not extend to a director who, without being at fault, has publicly declared his dissent to the carrying out of the act.

[74] Each quota holder of the company not participating in its management has the right to obtain information from the directors concerning the progress of the company's affairs, and to inspect the company's books (section 2476 of the Italian Civil Code).

[75] The by-laws provide the rules regarding the powers, authority and appointment of the statutory board of auditors or of the third-party auditor.

3.7 Controlling Body

[76] An important characteristic which is dissimilar from those of limited companies in common law countries is that all S.p.A.s, as well as S.r.l.s having certain characteristics, are subject to obligations which require the constitution of a controlling body.

[77] With regard to S.p.A.s, a board of statutory auditors (Collegio Sindacale), in addition to the normal board of directors (Consiglio di Amministrazione), or to the sole director (Amministratore Unico) must be appointed. The board of statutory auditors is composed, alternatively, of three to five permanent auditors pursuant to section 2397 of the Italian Civil Code. Two substitute auditors must also be appointed.

[78] The statutory auditors are appointed for the first time in the company's deed of incorporation and subsequently pursuant to a resolution of the shareholders' meeting; they remain in office for a period of three fiscal years up to the date of the shareholders' meeting convened for the approval of the financial statements relating to the third fiscal year of their office. They cannot be dismissed or revoked except for just cause. The remuneration of the statutory auditors, if not indicated in the by-laws, is decided by the shareholders' meeting, which appoints them for the entire duration of their office.

[79] The statutory auditors are responsible for verifying compliance of the corporate activities with the corporate law regulation and with the by-laws of the company, the fulfilment of the rules governing the management of the company and the adequacy of the governance, administrative and accounting structure of the company. The by-laws, in certain cases, may confer the accounting control function on the statutory auditors. In all other cases, the accounting control function must be performed by an auditor of an auditing company.

[80] The statutory auditors may, individually or collectively, carry out at any time acts of inspection and supervision on the company and may request information from the directors about the companies' activities and also specific information relating to controlled companies.

[81] The board of statutory auditors meets at least every ninety days and the auditors must attend shareholders' meetings and the board of directors' meetings as well as the executive committee's meetings.

[82] The statutory auditors have to fulfil their duties with the standard of ability and care required by the scope of their office; they are responsible for the soundness of their statements and must keep confidential any facts and documents of which they have knowledge by reason of their office. They are jointly liable, together with the directors, for acts and omissions of the directors when the damage would not have occurred had they exercised the proper degree of corporate control in compliance with the duties of their office.

[83] As far as S.r.l.s are concerned, the company may appoint a controlling body or an auditor. The controlling body may be represented either by a board of statutory auditors (in which case the provisions applicable to S.p.A.s will apply) or a sole statutory auditor. The possibility of appointing a board of statutory auditors must be expressly provided for by the by-laws of an S.r.l. However, if this option is not expressly selected, it is mandatory for the controlling body of the company to be represented by a sole statutory auditor.

[84] The appointment of a controlling body or of an auditor, in accordance with section 2477 of the Italian Civil Code, as amended by Decree Law No. 32 of 18 April 2019 (as implemented and modified by Law No. 55 of 14 June 2019), is mandatory (i) if the company is legally bound to prepare and file consolidated financial statements; (ii) if the company controls a company which is legally bound to the audit of its accounts; and (iii) if for two fiscal years two of the limits set out in the first paragraph of sections 2435*bis* of the Civil Code have been exceeded. The obligation ceases if, for three consecutive fiscal years, the above limits are not exceeded. The limits set out in sections 2435*bis* are: (a) total assets resulting from the annual accounts: EUR4 000 000; (b) revenues from sales and services: EUR4 000 000; and (c) an average number of staff employed during the fiscal year: twenty employees.

[85] Legislative Decree No. 58 of 24 February 1998 provides for new rules relating to the boards of statutory auditors of listed companies, granting each member of the board more effective powers of control over the company's management. Pursuant to section 151, any member of the board of statutory auditors may request the company's directors to provide information about the running of the company's business or about the way in which specific transactions have been performed; in addition, any member is entitled to carry out investigations into the management of the company. Furthermore, if the board of statutory auditors finds irregularities in the management of the company, then it must:

(a) report the facts to the shareholders' meeting (section 153 paragraph 1);
(b) notify the CONSOB of the violations which have been discovered and send them the minutes of the company's meetings, as well as any other useful documentation (section 149 paragraph 3);
(c) call a shareholders' meeting and a board of directors' meeting, as well as a meeting of the executive committee of the company (section 151 paragraph 2); and
(d) report the facts to the tribunal, pursuant to section 2409 of the Civil Code (section 152 paragraph 1).

[86] Otherwise, if the basis for suspicion of serious irregularities relates to the discharge of the duties of the statutory auditors (section 152 paragraph 2), the CONSOB is entitled to report those facts to the tribunal; costs and expenses incurred in relation to an investigation carried out by the CONSOB must be borne by the company.

3.8 The *Società a Responsabilità Limitata Semplificata*

[87] Law Decree No. 1 of 24 January 2012 (as implemented and modified by Law No. 27 of 24 March 2012) has introduced a sub-category of the S.r.l.: the Società a Responsabilità Limitata Semplificata (S.r.l.s.) – i.e., Simplified Limited Liability Company.

[88] The S.r.l.s., which is governed by the new sections 2463*bis* of the Italian Civil Code, has a corporate capital ranging from a minimum of EUR1.00 up to EUR9 999.99 and may be incorporated exclusively by natural persons. It benefits from (i) no stamp duty payable for the incorporation of the company, and (ii) certain simplifications compared with the legal structure of the standard S.r.l. However, it should be noted that a lesser degree of flexibility is provided with regard to the corporate governance of the S.r.l.s., as the by-laws of an S.r.l.s. must comply with the standard provided for by Ministerial Decree No. 138 of 23 June 2012 and may not be amended by the shareholders.

3.9 Provisions on Innovative Start-Up Companies

[89] With the issue of Article 25 of Law Decree No. 179 of 18 October 2012, as implemented by Law No. 221 of 17 December 2012, a regulatory framework was introduced into the Italian legal system aimed at developing the growth of new innovative companies, known as 'innovative start-ups'.

[90] Such innovative start-up companies may take the form of a corporation or a cooperative company, provided that the shares or quotas representing the company's capital are not listed on a regulated market or on a multilateral trading facility. Article 25 paragraph 2, of this Law Decree No. 179 provides for a series of formal and substantial requirements in order to be able to define a company as an 'innovative start-up'. In particular, (i) the company must have been incorporated and have been carrying on its business activity for no more than sixty months; (ii) the company must have a production headquarters or a branch in Italy; (iii) starting from the second year of activity, the company's total annual production value must not exceed EUR5 mn; (iv) the company must not distribute or have distributed profits; (v) the company's exclusive or primary corporate purpose must be the development, production and marketing of innovative products or services with a high technological value; (vi) the company must not have been incorporated through a merger, spin-off or following a transfer of a business or a branch of a business.

[91] In addition to the above, the innovative start-up must meet at least one of the following substantial requirements: (i) the research and development costs sustained by the company must be equal to or in excess of 15% of the production cost or the total value of the product itself (whichever greater); (ii) the company must hire as employees or consultants, to the extent of a percentage equal to or exceeding certain thresholds provided by the law, staff with certain academic qualifications or carrying out certain academic studies; (iii) the company must be the owner or consignee or licensee of certain intellectual property rights, or rights relating to computer programs, having certain characteristics provided by the law. Innovative start-ups meeting the requirements referred to above enjoy derogation from certain provisions of law which would normally apply to Italian companies, along with certain tax incentives.

Most innovative start-ups have chosen to be incorporated under the status of S.r.l. Although the S.r.l. was already by far the most commonly used company form for innovative Italian start-ups, the introduction of the new online procedure for incorporation of innovative start-ups (for which only this legal form is eligible), unquestionably increased this preference even further. In contrast, the introduction of the new procedure for incorporation led to a gradual decrease in the use of the simplified S.r.l. (S.r.l.s.). However, there are still a considerable number of innovative start-ups incorporated in this form. The remaining start-ups, accounting for less than 5% of the total, are cooperatives and S.p.A.s.

[92] The Legislator, with the introduction of the Law Decree No. 50 of 24 April 2017 (which was converted into the Law No. 96 of 21 June 2017), and of the Legislative Decree No. 129 of 3 August 2017 has extended to small- and medium-sized enterprises (SMEs) established in the form of an S.r.l. the exceptions to corporate law initially planned for 'innovative start-ups' since the end of 2012 and for 'innovative SMEs' since 2015 and specifically introduced the following options:

(a) the ability for quotas of SMEs-S.r.l. to derive from public offerings of financial products exploiting the equity crowd-funding instrument tool. Therefore SMEs in the form of limited liability companies and companies limited by shares are treated the same as regards their respective possibilities of addressing the public in order to acquire the necessary capital for their entrepreneurial activity;
(b) the ability to provide, in the deed of incorporation of SMEs-S.r.l., particular categories of quota having different rights and, (within limits imposed by the law), to freely determine the content of the different categories;(c) the ability to provide, in the deed of incorporation of SMEs-S.r.l., categories of quotas that do not carry any voting rights, or which attribute to the quotaholder voting rights which are not proportional to the quotaholding held by it.

In light of the above, the Italian Legislator has by this reform fragmented the legal framework on limited liability companies, separating into a twin-track those limited liability companies which do fall within the definition of SMEs and those which do not (effectively meaning those with more than 250 employees), to which the prohibition provided by Article 2468 of the Italian Civil Code will continue to apply.

4 TRANSFER OF CONTROL

[93] Essentially, there are three possible ways of transferring the ownership of an enterprise: (1) the sale of the equity of a company; (2) the sale of its assets as a going concern; and (3) the merger of one company with another.

4.1 Sale of Equity

[94] The sale of equity of an Italian company is quite straightforward, and the practice is in many ways similar to that in other major European countries. It is worth noting that in the case of a sale of shares, the legal entity remains unaffected; what occurs is a change in the identity of the owners, thus leaving all the legal relationships of the company itself (including those with the company's employees) unaffected.

[95] In principle, the equity of a company is freely transferable as from the time the company is duly registered in the relevant Register of Companies. Restrictions on the freedom of transfer may be provided for by specific provisions of the Italian law or by the company's by-laws. Restrictions on the sale of interests in a company which are agreed upon by the shareholders and which are not reflected in the by-laws (e.g., lock-up provisions contained in shareholders' agreements) are valid and enforceable, but only between the parties to such agreements and do not affect the company itself or bona fide third parties.

[96] With regard to the manner/method of transfer of equity interests, a distinction must be drawn between companies whose interests are represented by shares (among which the S.p.A.s) and companies whose interests are represented by quotas (among which the S.r.l.s). In particular, as regards companies whose interests are represented by shares a further distinction may be drawn between those companies whose shares are represented by share certificates and those companies (in particular, listed companies) whose shares are represented only by book entries (azioni dematerializzate).

[97] Interests which are represented by share certificates may be transferred either through (i) the endorsement of the share certificates in favour of the purchaser, undersigned by the seller and certified by a Notary Public, or (ii) an annotation of the transfer on the relevant share certificates made by a director of the company, on the basis of a transfer deed certified by a Notary Public (so-called transfer). The transfer must also be recorded by a director in the shareholders' ledger (libro soci) of the company.

[98] A transfer of interests represented by quotas must be carried out by execution of a deed which must be certified by a Notary Public.

[99] The transfer of the shares of listed companies represented by book entries (azioni dematerializzate) is carried out through a centralized depositary of the shares with a management company (so-called società di gestione accentrata), through book entries.

[100] In some cases, however, the acquisition of a controlling or minority interest in a company may be realized through a tender offer on the market. This is the case in the acquisition of controlling or minority interest in listed companies. For the specific regulation and procedure applying to such cases, please *see* the section 5 'Tender Offers' below.

[101] Normally the acquisition of an interest in a company is managed through the execution of a purchase and sale agreement (as the case may be, of the company's shares or quotas), on the basis of a negotiation with the relevant shareholders. Very often, due to the need to carry out certain activities in the interim, the signing and the closing of the transaction are not simultaneous. In these cases, the purchase and sale agreement is represented by a preliminary agreement under Italian law, which establishes two separate obligations: respectively, the obligation of the seller to sell the equity interest and the obligation of the buyer to purchase the equity interest and to pay the purchase price, upon fulfilment of certain pre-closing conditions. Typical examples of such pre-closing conditions might include the need to obtain certain authorizations from public bodies (for instance, antitrust clearances), the need to obtain waivers from third parties (for instance, financing banks or contractual counterparts), satisfactory completion of due diligence processes, the execution of specific agreements in the interim period, etc.

[102] Agreements for the acquisition of interests in a company through private negotiations normally contain representations and warranties from the seller(s). The most common representations and warranties requested by the purchaser relates to ownership of the interest sold, as well as financial, corporate, tax, labour and social security, intellectual property, litigation, environmental and other matters. Acquisition agreements may also include specific indemnification obligations undertaken by the seller in favour of the purchaser if losses, contingencies or liabilities are suffered by the purchaser (or by the target company) as a consequence of one or more of such representations and warranties proving not to be true. In practice, the duration of most such representations and warranties usually ranges from one to three years, while for representations and warranties relating to ownership of the interest sold, labour and social security, tax and environmental issues, a longer duration is often agreed.

[103] In addition, agreements relating to the acquisition of a controlling interest in a company often contain certain non-competition or non-solicitation obligations, whereby the seller undertakes to abstain from carrying on the same or a similar business to that of the target company or to hire employees from the target company for a certain period of time. It must be noted that, under Italian law, a specific consideration in favour of the seller for the grant of such undertakings should be agreed.

4.2 Sale of Assets (Going Concern)

[104] Apart from buying stock, the remaining choices for securing an immediate involvement in Italian commerce or industry lie in the purchase of a business as a going concern or in a merger with another company. One advantage of purchasing a business as a going concern compared to the purchase of equity is the fact that the purchaser limits its risk as regards contingent liabilities relating to the relevant going concern. As against the purchase of a controlling interest in a company, where the purchaser assumes liability (at least, indirectly) for all the obligations and liabilities of the company of which the purchaser has acquired control.

[105] The purchase of a business as going concern is regulated by the provisions of sections 2555 et seq. of the Italian Civil Code. First, Italian law defines the 'going concern' as the bulk of the goods (and legal relationships) organized by the entrepreneur for the exercise of an economic activity. Therefore, as a consequence of the transfer of the going concern, all such goods and legal relationships (and related debts and credits) as part of the going concern are transferred to the purchaser, who consequently acquires legal title to all of them. The elements of a going concern may include (and usually include), by way of example, inventory, trademarks, patents or other intellectual property rights, employees, real property or rights to use real property (including leases and tenancy agreements, etc.), contracts and so on.

[106] When ownership of a going concern is transferred, the claims and accounts receivable relating to the going concern are usually transferred to the purchaser. Recorded liabilities, for which the seller remains jointly liable, are also usually transferred to the acquirer, but any hidden or contingent liabilities remain the responsibility of the seller unless the agreement provides otherwise. Moreover, there is no specific requirement that debtors of the going concern have to be notified of the sale, and all agreements of a non-personal nature are automatically transferred without the need for the consent of the other parties. However, some protection is given to the latter group, in that counterparties to contracts have three months in which to terminate the agreement on the grounds of 'just cause'.

[107] When a business is sold as a going concern, the contracts with employees are also transferred, and in the case of certain collective agreements, union approval might, in fact, be a prerequisite. When more than fifteen employees are involved, the proposed sale must be communicated to the unions at least twenty-five days in advance.

[108] Especially where staff reductions are envisaged, it would be inadvisable to proceed without consideration of the union position, given that the unions enjoy a powerful and protected status in Italy. It is also important to be aware that pursuant to section 2112 of the Italian Civil Code, the seller and the purchaser of a going concern are jointly liable for all benefits and receivables to which the employees were entitled at the time of the transfer. To free the seller from such liability, specific agreements need to be reached with the employees, it is understood that to be effective such agreements have to be executed before a union or before specific public offices.

[109] Another kind of joint liability of the seller and the purchaser is established by Italian Law in relation to tax liabilities. However, Legislative Decree No. 472 of 18

December 1997 has introduced the right to ask the competent tax offices for a cer tificate stating all the tax liabilities relating to the going concern in question. Where such certificates are requested, the potential tax liability of the purchaser is limitec to the amount stated in the relevant certificate (and no liability will apply in the event the certificate is not issued by the tax authorities within forty days from the request).

[110] The transfer of a going concern is carried out through the execution of a transfer deed, which needs to be executed in writing and to be certified by a Notary Public. In addition, the deed must be recorded in the competent Companies Reg ister. It is very common to provide, in the context of deeds for the transfer of going concerns, a set of representations and warranties of the seller, which are broadly in line with those already described above for the sale and purchase of equity inter ests.

4.3 Mergers and Spin-Offs

[111] These considerations should be contrasted with the case of mergers, where all liabilities (including hidden and contingent liabilities) are automatically trans ferred, and where the creditors of the two companies enjoy the benefit of specific statutory protection. The merger will automatically be stayed for two months, in order for a decision to be made by the creditors as to whether they wish to file an objection before the courts. The courts possess a wide discretion to decide on any such objection and may require the provision of guarantees or may decide that the merger can take place notwithstanding the objection. If, however, the creditor approve the transaction, or appropriate amounts are deposited with a credit insti tution by way of guarantee in favour of the creditors, the opportunity will then arise for a so-called fast merger to take place. Under this procedure, the requirement of a delay for the two-month period is removed. It is also worth noting that, in the case of a merger, holders of convertible bonds may exercise their rights of conver sion.

[112] As far as 'spin-offs' (*Scissione*) of companies are concerned, section 2506 of the Italian Civil Code provides for two types of spin-off: the first type is effected by means of transfer from one company of all its assets to two or more companies – whether companies to be incorporated or already existing – ('de-merger' or *scis sione totale*); the second type is effected by means of transfer of part of the compa ny's assets (*scissione parziale*). The basic difference between the two types of spin-off is that in the first case, the company ceases to exist after the transfer has been per formed, while in the second, the company remains in existence but with a decreased capital. Both in the first and in the second type, a detailed description of the assets to be transferred as well as any other information related to the spin-of procedure must be set out in the relevant project. It is not proposed to enter into details of the spin-off procedure here; suffice it to say that it basically follows the merger procedure. One type of merger is carried out by the creation of a single new company resulting from the merger of two separate companies, which then cease to exist. The other type, which is used more frequently, is where a company incorporates into itself one or more other companies, which are then extinguished. The merger must be the subject of a resolution in the course of an extraordinary shareholders' meeting of each company involved; however, according to sections 2505 and 2505*bis* of the Italian Civil Code, the resolution of the company that is going to incorporate the other company can be passed by the board of directors in the event that the incorporating company already owns at least 90% of the incorporated company provided this procedure is set out in the by-laws. This resolution must then be registered in the Companies' Register and must be accompanied by:

(a) a description of the merger project, setting out all the main aspects of the companies involved and the consequences of the merger;
(b) a statement of assets and liabilities of the companies participating in the merger (as this has to be presented to the shareholders in cases where their resolution is required) as at a date within the preceding four months;
(c) a report of the board of directors about the economic and legal profile of the merger and about the proposed exchange ratio of the shares;
(d) an audit report, drawn up by an expert, relating to the adequacy of the exchange ratio of the shares proposed by the directors.

[113] Following the statutory two-month period (or a shorter period of time in the case of a fast merger), the merger can be legally implemented by the drawing up of a public deed of the merger by an Italian notary public.

[114] Thus, the role of the courts is limited, on the one hand, to the exercise of a wide discretion following an objection by a creditor within the two-month period (which can be thwarted by depositing the relevant amount in a bank), and, on the other hand, to the verification that all the correct procedures have been scrupulously followed. Should there be indications of violations of other aspects of company law, such as a conflict of interest or breach of a director's duty, alternative court actions would have to be taken. In such circumstances, the court would have wide power to nullify the transactions concerned.

[115] In order to give some protection to shareholders and to promote transparency in the share market, legislation was passed in 1974 which established the CONSOB, and which, *inter alia*, contained important provisions relating to mergers. Pursuant to section 70 of the CONSOB Regulation No. 11971/99, certain formalities must be complied with by listed companies involved in a merger (or de-merger) transaction: thirty days before the date scheduled for the shareholders' meeting called in order to approve the merger, certain documents such as the merger project, the report of the proposed merger, as well as the statements of assets and liabilities of the companies involved in the merger, must be delivered to the CONSOB, or publicized by different means indicated by the Law and, in addition, must be deposited at the company's registered office. Furthermore, thirty days after the shareholders' meeting has been held, the minutes of the meeting, as well as the resolutions adopted, must be notified to the CONSOB, or publicized by different means indicated by the Law. A copy of the merger deed must be delivered to the CONSOB, or publicized as above, within ten days of filing with the relevant Register of Companies.

4.4 Legal Requirements in Chronological Sequence for a Merger by Incorporation

[116] We summarize, in this section below, an example of a hypothetical merger, according to standard terms, to give a practical idea of the requirements and the timing to carry out a merger transaction in Italy. The incorporating company is represented by J. The incorporated company is represented by K. The date for the start of the transaction is indicated by X. The figures refer to the estimated number of days for the accomplishment of each formality (without taking into account abbreviation of terms which may occur in specific circumstances and antitrust provisions).

[117] J/X: Meeting of the board of directors in order to propose the merger of K into J and to call, as provided by law, the extraordinary shareholders' meeting which will resolve the merger. Preparation of:

- the description of the merger project;
- the report of the directors; and
- the statement of assets and liabilities of the company as at a date not more than four months prior to the day on which such statement will be deposited at the company's registered office or published on its website; this statement can be substituted by the annual balance sheet, if this relates to a date, not more than six months prior to the date of the above deposit or publication.

K/X: Meeting of the board of directors in order to examine the merger proposal and to call the shareholders' meeting of the company (extraordinary shareholders' meeting in the case of an S.p.A.) which will resolve the merger. Preparation of the same documents as above.

X+15: Report of an expert, who/which in some cases has to be appointed by the tribunal, on the adequacy of the proposed exchange ratio of the shares.

X+15+5: The description of the merger project, the report of the directors, the statement of assets and liabilities (or the annual balance sheet), the report of the expert and the balance sheets of all the companies involved for the last three years are filed with the registered office of such companies or published on their websites.

J/X+15+5+30: At least thirty days after the filing of the said documents, the extraordinary shareholders' meeting is held to resolve the incorporation of K and to approve the related terms and conditions, as well as to grant all the necessary powers to the directors for the execution of the deed of the merger.

K/X+15+5+30: At least thirty days after the filing of the said documents, the extraordinary shareholders' meeting is held to resolve the merger into J and to approve the related terms and conditions, as well as to grant all the necessary powers to the directors for the execution of the deed of the merger.

J/X+15+5+30+15: Filing of the merger resolution adopted by the extraordinary shareholders' meeting of the company with the relevant Companies' Register.

K/X+15+5+30+15: Filing of the merger resolution adopted by the extraordinary shareholders' meeting with the relevant Companies' Register.

X+15+5+30+15+5+60: At least sixty days after the latest filing of the merger resolution with the Register of Companies, the deed of merger can be signed, provided that during such period no creditor of the companies involved has notified his objection to the merger.

K/X+15+5+30+15+5+60+10: The deed of the merger is filed with the Companies' Register, where the incorporated company has its own registered office.

J/X+15+5+30+15+5+60+15: The deed of the merger is filed with the Register of Companies of competent jurisdiction for the incorporating company. From this moment, the merger takes effect. The time usually required from start to finish is approximately five months, without taking into account the time necessary to prepare the initial documentation.

4.5 Regulatory Bodies

4.5.1 CONSOB (*Commissione Nazionale per le Società e la Borsa*: Stock Exchange Authority)

[118] With regard to mergers and acquisitions, the main regulatory body in Italy is the CONSOB, which is the Italian stock exchange regulatory authority. Such authority was introduced by Law No. 216 of 7 June 1974 and is aimed to protect and guarantee the regular and correct operation of the stock market, the completeness and accuracy of information that must be mandatorily disclosed to investors and the completeness and accuracy of the facts stated to investors in prospectuses related to offerings of transferable securities.

[119] CONSOB is a public law body which has regulatory independence with regard to the matters reserved to it.

[120] CONSOB is composed of five members appointed by the President of the Republic on the basis of a proposal by the Prime Minister. The members of the CONSOB hold office for seven years and may not be re-appointed.

[121] The powers and functions of the CONSOB have been constantly increased and include the following:

- the regulation of the institution, organization and operation of the financial markets;
- the regulation of the activity of intermediaries authorized to operate on the financial markets;
- the information obligations of companies listed on financial markets;
- the authorization of public offers for sale of financial instruments (including IPOs), tender offers, and in general any form of solicitation to investors.

4.5.2 Bank of Italy

[122] Where banks are involved, the Bank of Italy plays an important supervisory role. Its authorization must be sought and obtained prior to the merger, spin-off or transfer of ownership of any bank. Moreover, certain rules regulate the proportion of equity that a bank may own in a company which operates in a sphere unrelated to banking – and, equally importantly, vice versa.

[123] Moreover, where State-owned banks considered to be of national interest are concerned, an acquisition by a non-EC national could be subject to severe restrictions.

4.5.3 IVASS

[124] The insurance industry also suffers close regulation. For mergers and takeovers in this sector, the prior authorization of the IVASS (*Istituto per la Vigilanza sulle Assicurazioni*, formerly named ISVAP, *Istituto per la Vigilanza sulle Assicurazioni Private*), the regulatory and supervisory agency for the insurance sector, must be obtained. Upon consolidation, the new company emerging from the transaction is under an obligation to seek the requisite insurance license.

5 TENDER OFFERS

[125] Legislative Decree No. 58 of 24 February 1998, as subsequently amended and supplemented (the Financial Services Acts (FSA)), contains specific provisions regarding the procedure for and the regulation of public bids. The provisions of the FSA are supplemented by Regulation No. 11971 issued by CONSOB on 14 May 1999, as amended and supplemented (the 'CONSOB Regulation').

[126] According to section 120 of the FSA, any owner of more than 3% of the voting shares of a listed company must give notice of such shareholding to CONSOB and to the relevant company.

[127] As far as public purchase offers or exchange bids are concerned (Offerte Pubbliche di Acquisto o di Scambio or OPAs), section 1 paragraph 1(v) of the FSA defines a public purchase or exchange bid as any 'offer, invitation to offer or promotional message – in whatever form it is made – aimed at the purchase or the exchange of financial products'.

[128] Section 102 of the FSA provides a specific procedure for the implementation of a public purchase or exchange bid.

[129] If a public purchase or exchange bid is planned or becomes mandatory by law, the bidder must give prompt notice of the bid to CONSOB, to the Stock Exchange (Borsa Italiana S.p.A.) and to the target company. As soon as the bid has been made public in the manner indicated above, the board of directors of the target company and of the bidder must inform their respective works councils, or (if no works council is in place) their employees, about the bid. Within twenty days from the date on which the bid has been made public, the bidder must launch the bid, by filing with CONSOB a prospectus (documento d'offerta), to be drafted in accordance with CONSOB's requirements. In case of failure to file the prospectus with CONSOB within the said term of twenty days, the prospectus will be rejected, and the bidder will be prevented from making a bid in respect of financial instruments issued by the same target company for the following period of twelve months.

[130] CONSOB will approve the prospectus within fifteen days of receiving it if it deems that it is sufficient to enable the public to evaluate the bid. When approving the prospectus, CONSOB may also require the bidder to disclose additional information or to comply with specific formalities for the publication of the prospectus, as well as to provide surety for the fulfilment of its obligations deriving from the bid. As soon as CONSOB has given its approval, the prospectus (together with any additional information which CONSOB may have required the bidder to disclose) must be notified to the target company and published. As soon as the prospectus has been published, the board of directors of the target company and that of the bidder must make it available to their respective works councils, or (if no works council is in place) to their employees.

[131] While a bid is in progress, CONSOB may suspend it if there is any ground for suspicion that any breaches of the provisions of the FSA or of the CONSOB Regulation have been committed.

[132] If it is subsequently proved that such breaches have indeed been committed, CONSOB may definitively stop the bid. CONSOB may also suspend the bid for no longer than thirty days in case of occurrence of new circumstances (or, in any event, of circumstances not previously disclosed and which are such as to prevent the public from being able to evaluate the bid).

[133] The board of directors of the target company must release a notice, which must contain the information necessary to enable the shareholders to evaluate the bid, and in which the board of directors must express its opinion on the bid, with specific reference to the effects of the bid on the target company, the prospects for its employees and the localization of production sites. This notice must be notified to the target company's works council or (if no works council is in place) to its employees.

[134] As a rule, the CONSOB Regulation provides for a term of duration of the bid from fifteen to forty-five days. The CONSOB Regulation also provides specific rules regarding the amendment of the terms of a bid or the launching of competitive bids.

[135] One of the most interesting aspects of public purchase or exchange bids is the analysis of defensive strategies, by means of which the target company may try to counter a bid. The most common devices for countering a bid include the purchase by the target company of its own shares (subject to the conditions provided by the law), a merger or a spin-off, a capital increase, the issuing of bonds convertible into shares, the purchase of holdings in other companies. The FSA limits the possibility to take defensive steps in several respects. In particular, section 104 of the

FSA provides that, while a purchase or exchange bid is pending, the target company must refrain from taking any steps which might prejudice the outcome of the bid (the so-called passivity rule) unless such steps were expressly authorized by a resolution of the meeting of the shareholders. Such restriction had been abolished by Law Decree No. 185 of 29 November 2008 but was then reinstated by Legislative Decree No. 146 of 25 September 2009. The version of section 104 of the FSA currently in force provides in any case for the ability, for Italian listed companies, to derogate, in their by-laws, from the passivity rule.

[136] Sections 104*bis* of the FSA provides that the so-called neutralization rule (whereby any restrictions on voting rights, as well as any restrictions on the transfer of shares, provided by the by-laws of the target company or by any agreement between its shareholders, are deemed to be ineffective during any period set for the acceptance of the bid) is a mere option or faculty that the target company may choose to implement in its by-laws.

[137] Sections 106 and 108 of the FSA outline the circumstances under which a public purchase or exchange bid is mandatory. Pursuant to section 106 of the FSA, a public bid for the purchase of all of the voting shares of a listed company must be made within twenty days by any person who, as a result of one or more purchases, now holds more than 30% of the voting shares (or of the voting rights) of such company. If such holding of more than 30% of the voting shares of a listed company has been acquired by persons acting in concert, all those persons will be obliged, jointly and severally, to make the said purchase bid.

[138] Decree Law No. 91 of 24 June 2014, as subsequently converted into Law No. 116 of 11 August 2014, sets out certain cases in which the 30% threshold referred to above is reduced to 25%.

[139] For the sake of completeness, section 1 paragraph 1 (w-quarter.1) of the FSA provides for the definition of SMEs in relation to listed shares. SMEs with listed shares are those companies which have a market capitalization below EUR500 000 000.00. Under section 106 paragraph 1*bis* of the FSA, any such SMEs are entitled to modify their by-laws by introducing a threshold for mandatory public purchase or exchange bids between 25% and 40%.

[140] The purchase price for each class of shares must be no lower than the highest price paid by the bidder (or by any person acting in concert with the bidder) for the purchase of shares of the same class in the preceding twelve-month period. If no purchase has been made of shares of the relevant class during such period, the purchase price must be no lower than the weighted average of the quoted market prices of such class of shares during the said twelve-month period. Section 106 of the FSA provides that, under certain circumstances, the purchase price may be fixed by CONSOB at a higher or lower level. The consideration offered by the bidder may also consist, in whole or in part, of shares or other securities (as a general rule, these securities would also be listed in a regulated market).

[141] Section 106 of the FSA provides for a number of exemptions from the obligation to make the mandatory bid described above, where a holding of more than

30% of the voting shares of a listed company has been acquired (a) through a previous public bid for the purchase of all of the voting shares of such listed company; or (b) in the context of the process of reorganization of a listed company in financial difficulty; or (c) from a seller belonging to the same group of companies as the purchaser; or (d) for reasons not depending on the will of the purchaser; or (e) as a temporary step; or (f) in the context of a merger or spin-off transaction; or (g) for no consideration.

[142] An additional exemption from the obligation to make the mandatory bid described above is provided by section 107 of the FSA, in the event that a holding of more than 30% of the voting shares of a listed company has been acquired through a previous public bid for the purchase of at least 60% of the voting shares of such listed company, provided however that CONSOB is satisfied that (a) neither the purchaser, nor any person acting in concert with the purchaser, has acquired more than 1% of the voting shares of such listed company during the preceding twelve-month period, and (b) that the previous bid had been made conditional upon the approval of a number of shareholders holding the majority of the voting shares of such listed company (excluding any shares held by the bidder himself, or by the majority shareholder, or by persons related to them).

[143] Pursuant to section 108 of the FSA, a public bid for the purchase of all of the remaining voting shares of a listed company must be made by any bidder who, as a result of a mandatory bid for the purchase of all of the voting shares of such listed company, has acquired not less than 95% of the voting shares of such company. Without prejudice to the above, any person who comes to hold more than 90% of the voting shares of a listed company must make a public offer for the purchase of all of the remaining voting shares of such listed company unless a sufficient number of floating shares is restored within a period of ninety days, such as to permit regular market dealings of such shares. If the said holding of at least 95% (or more than 90%, as the case may be) of the voting shares of a listed company has been acquired by persons acting in concert, all those persons will be obliged, jointly and severally, to make the said purchase offer.

[144] The purchase price, in the event that the said holding of at least 95% (or more than 90%, as the case may be) has been acquired exclusively through a public bid for the purchase of all of the voting shares of the relevant listed company, must equal the purchase price offered by the bidder in the previous public bid. Otherwise, the purchase price will be fixed by CONSOB, taking into account the market price in the preceding six months as well as the price offered by the bidder in the previous public bid.

[145] Pursuant to section 111 of the FSA, a bidder who, as a result of a mandatory bid for the purchase of all of the voting shares of a listed company, comes to hold more than 95% of the voting shares of such listed company, has the right to purchase all of the remaining voting shares of such listed company, within a period of three months after the expiry of the term for acceptance of the previous bid, provided, however, that he has expressed his intention to exercise such right in the prospectus relating to the previous bid.

6 HOSTILE TAKEOVERS

[146] As we have seen, the fact that few Italian companies have the majority of their voting stock publicly traded, coupled with the high degree of influence exercised by the State in the economy, reduces the number of potential targets for hostile bids. Moreover, certain aspects of Italian law can be used to erect obstacles to such bids. These are of different use and effect.

[147] An effective instrument for retaining a close hold over the transfer of ownership of the shares of a limited company is to create options or rights of first refusal.

[148] These may take the form either of terms in a shareholders' agreement or provisions in the by-laws of a company. The former, as a contract between shareholders, is of limited use because it is binding only on the contracting parties. Thus, it cannot block a sale of the shares but will only give rise to a claim for damages. A provision in the by-laws is more effective as the requirement must be met for any transfer to be considered valid. The difficulty, in practice, lies in the fact that such changes must be resolved in the course of an extraordinary shareholders' meeting which requires, as a minimum, an absolute majority of votes (and possibly more, should the relevant by-laws so require). Similar considerations arise in relation to the so-called super-majority provisions. These, according to the legal opinion, are effective with respect to extraordinary shareholders' meetings and may, therefore, be significant in relation to mergers and acquisitions, as will be seen below. It seems that in the context of ordinary shareholders' meetings, they are of doubtful legal validity.

[149] Legislative Decree No. 58 of 24 February 1998 introduced new provisions relating to shareholders' agreements of listed companies. Under the provisions of section 122, shareholders' agreements relating to the exercise of voting rights, within five days from their execution, must (a) be notified to CONSOB; (b) be published in abstract in the most important daily press, (c) be filed in the relevant Companies' Register, and (d) be notified to the companies whose shares are listed. Failure to comply with all such formalities will render the shareholders' agreement null and void and the exercise of voting rights will be suspended.

[150] In addition, the provisions contained in section 122 are applied to those shareholders' agreements that, among other things, require prior consultation for the exercise of voting rights or limitations on the transfer of shares or equities.

[151] Pursuant to section 123, shareholders' agreements with time limits must not exceed three years and will be regarded as having a three-year duration even if the parties provided for a longer term. In circumstances where the shareholders' agreement has no time limit, each party may withdraw by giving six months' notice.

[152] A significant novelty of the corporate law reform is the introduction of provisions relating to shareholders' agreements applicable to non-listed companies. In particular, sections 2341*bis* of the Italian Civil Code stipulate that shareholders' agreements which (a) regulate the exercise of voting rights; and/or (b) introduce limits to the transfer of the shares, must have a maximum duration of five years.

[153] One possible tactic is to provide the board of directors, by a resolution passed at an extraordinary shareholders' meeting, with an entitlement to increase the corporate capital at any time in the course of a given period (not exceeding five years). Without such a provision, the timetable required to increase the capital would render such a tactic ineffective in the face of any hostile bid.

[154] The purchase by a company of its own shares is illegal except in certain limited circumstances. A duly called shareholders' meeting must approve the resolution and the amount of consideration to be paid may not exceed the total of the unrestricted reserves and undistributed profits. A purchase by a subsidiary would also be subject to the same limitations.

[155] Pursuant to section 132 of Legislative Decree No. 58 of 24 February 1998, purchases of treasury shares must be made by listed companies so as to ensure equal treatment of the shareholders, according to procedures established by CONSOB. The same provision is applied in the event that a controlled company (as defined by section 2359 of the Civil Code) purchases shares of its listed parent company.

[156] In any event with regard to companies listed on the Stock Exchange or on the over-the-counter market, Legislative Decree No. 58 of 24 February 1998 is now applicable. This law establishes, *inter alia*, an obligation on the party intending to acquire control over such a company to proceed by means of a takeover bid; the objective being to obtain better protection for minority shareholders and more transparency for the entire transaction. A more thorough examination of Italian law on takeover bids is made above.

[157] Finally, it should be noted that any sale of, or option granted over, the stock or the most significant assets held by a company with a view to discouraging potential takeover bids might subsequently be scrutinized by the court, upon application by the shareholders, to ascertain whether there has been a breach of fiduciary duty on the part of the directors or perhaps a conflict of interest between the directors and the company. Should a court be satisfied that a conflict of interest has occurred, and where potential prejudice to the company has been demonstrated, the court may declare that the sale or option is legally invalid.

[158] However, it cannot do so if this would prejudice the rights of third parties acting in good faith.

7 ANTITRUST/COMPETITION ISSUES

[159] The Italian antitrust law (Law No. 287 of 10 October 1990) was implemented by a regulation contained in the Decree of the President of the Republic No. 461 of 10 September 1991, concerning the powers of investigation and the duty of secrecy of the Italian Competition and Market Authority. The aim of this legislation is to minimize or prevent situations which restrict or eliminate competition. It is designed to supplement the EU competition laws and hence governs only to the extent that the EU laws are inapplicable.

[160] The legislation essentially considers freedom of competition within three categories of activity: transactions which result in a concentration of market power, abuses of dominant market positions and agreements restricting free competition. In order to supervise, investigate and enforce compliance with the relevant provisions of Italian law, a Competition and Market Authority was established (the 'Authority'). It is independent and appointed by the speakers of the two Houses of Parliament.

[161] It is specifically provided by the Authority that the regulations and case law of the EU may be used for purposes of interpretation. From the point of view of mergers and acquisitions, the most relevant provision concerns operations of concentration. Transactions which are considered operations of concentration are defined as those in which two or more enterprises merge, or in which one or more parties which already control another entity acquire control (as defined) of a third entity, directly or indirectly, through share purchase, assets purchase or any other means, or in which two or more entities consolidate through the creation of a new enterprise. The assumption of control of an enterprise by a bank or a financial institution under certain specified circumstances is expressly exempted from the application of this Section. In addition, transactions in which the purpose and principal effect is the coordination of the behaviour of independent entities are not considered operations of concentration.

[162] As of 2021, when there is an operation of concentration and (i) the aggregate domestic turnover of all the enterprises involved amounts to at least EUR511 000 000, and (ii) the domestic revenue of the company to be acquired exceeds EUR31 000 000, the undertaking concerned is bound to notify the concentration to the Authority in order that the latter should be in a position to review the impact of the transaction on market concentration. Until the end of 2012, the two thresholds referred to above were alternative (i.e., if only one of them was exceeded the obligation to notify the concentration was triggered). Instead, now the obligation to notify the concentration is triggered only in the event that both of the aforesaid thresholds are exceeded. The relevant thresholds are to be indexed yearly in line with inflation.

[163] The Authority must, within thirty days, launch an investigation if it believes that the proposed transaction may result in the creation or strengthening of a dominant position in the domestic market such as substantially to reduce competition. If no investigation is launched within this period, the concentration is deemed cleared.

[164] Such situations are to be assessed in the light of possible choices available to suppliers and end-users, the market position of the relevant entities, their access to sources of supply and to market outlets, the structure of the market, the competitive situation of the national industry, barriers to entry of the relevant market and the supply and demand trend for the products or services in question.

[165] The Authority has the power to suspend the transaction for the period of inquiry, which may not last more than forty-five days. At the end of the investigation, a transaction may be approved, or enjoined, or approved subject to the prescription of any measures considered necessary to restore actual competition. To give the Authority effective power, there are provisions for vigorous financial sanctions in the face of failure to provide information, the provision of insufficient or false information or lack of compliance.

[166] As far as banks are concerned, their turnover is deemed to equal one-tenth of the value of the assets referred to in the statement of assets and liabilities, less the value of what is referred to in the antitrust law as the 'Conti d'Ordine'. For the insurance industry, turnover is considered in terms of the premiums collected in the course of the year in question.

[167] In the case of a tender offer, the enterprises concerned must notify to the Authority simultaneously, together with the notification, they are also required to make to the CONSOB. The Authority is obliged to make a decision as to whether to investigate within the following fifteen days and to complete any such investigation within forty-five days from its start.

[168] Should the operation be completed before the end of the investigation, the Authority, instead of reversing the sale, may remove voting rights and order the divestiture of assets or order the taking of any such measures as it considers necessary to restore competition.

[169] In the event that transactions which result in a concentration of market power, abuses of dominant market positions and agreements restricting free competition concern companies operating in sectors subject to the supervision of more than one authority, each of them may adopt the measures within its competence.

[170] Finally, there are two rights conferred on the government under section 25. First, it is expressly empowered to permit any transaction that would otherwise be struck down for excessive concentration, where there are exceptional countervailing reasons pertaining to the national economy. Second, where a party to the transaction is a national of another country which does not afford reciprocal trade rights to those offered by the Italian legislation, the government may prohibit a transaction which would otherwise be valid, on the grounds of 'reasons essential to the national economy'.

[171] The precise time when notification of a contemplated transaction exceeding the financial threshold (and hence within the scope of the provisions) must be given to the Authority is not specifically laid down and may, therefore, give rise to uncertainty. The statute merely states that 'operations of concentration must be communicated to the Authority in advance'. Given that a merger transaction is technically not completed until the production of certain notarial documents, and bearing in mind that the Authority has thirty days to examine the concentration, it could be argued that the notification would have to be given around forty days before the date scheduled for completion of the deal.

[172] The two other areas on which the antitrust law (Law No. 287/1990) focuse are less obviously relevant to mergers and acquisitions. They make no reference t any financial threshold and, therefore, cover the entire scope of the market.

[173] Section 2 prohibits agreements of any kind which have as their object o effect the prevention, restriction or distortion of competition in the relevant secto of the national market. This part of the antitrust law is aimed more directly a agreements which, for example, fix prices, limit or restrict production, market outlets, investment, technological developments or technical progress, or which divid the market or sources of supply or where agreements apply dissimilar conditions t equivalent trading transactions such that unjust competitive advantages ar obtained. Under certain circumstances, an argument could perhaps be maintaine that a transaction falling outside section 5 (because it is below the relevant financia threshold) could be construed as an agreement distorting competition pursuant t section 2 and, hence, comes within the grasp of the Authority's powers.

[174] Similar considerations must be applied to a third area of the antitrust law Section 3 is concerned with activities which are construed by the Authority as a abuse of a dominant market position. The activities expressly forbidden by this section are substantially identical to those referred to in section 2 in relation to restrictive agreements. Considering that the antitrust law makes no attempt to defin 'dominant position', nor does it limit the range of activities which might be considered an abuse of such position, the interpretations of EU law in this area will be relevant. Again, it appears to be arguable that simply by effecting a merger o acquisition, an entity may be committing an act that, in itself, could be construed a an abuse of a dominant position.

[175] The Authority may make inquiries under both sections 2 and 3 on the basi of public knowledge or information from interested parties or on the basis of general reviews of various sectors of the national economy.

[176] Last but not least, the 'Golden Power' regulations (Law Decree No. 21 of 1 March 2012, as implemented by Law No. 56 of 11 May 2012): the term 'Golde Power' (as it is called in Italy, in other countries it is referred to as 'foreign investment control' or 'screening') is a set of special powers that the Italian Governmen can exercise (i) to impose specific conditions in case of purchase, by a foreign company, of shareholdings in Italian companies which are strategic or active in a secto that is considered fundamental or (ii) to veto the adoption of resolutions relating t extraordinary or particularly important transactions that could compromis national interests. Over time, the sectors identified as strategic have bee expanded to include the following areas: finance, credit, insurance, energy, transportation, health, food safety, artificial intelligence and cybersecurity.

[177] Therefore, in case, for example, of mergers or acquisitions likely to affect th ownership of assets considered to be strategic, there is an obligation to notify th Presidency of the Council of Ministers in order to allow it to carry out its inspectio activities. Notification must be made within ten days of completion of the transaction and the Government has forty-five days to express its opinion or request an clarifications. If the Government does not express its opinion within the abov period, the transaction is understood to have been authorized. It is also possible to submit a pre-notification for a preliminary examination of the applicability of the golden power regulations and the admissibility of the transaction.

8 FINANCE: LEVERAGED BUYOUTS

[178] In order to finance a merger or acquisition, the popular concept of a leveraged buyout, as frequently used in the US and in the UK, has been used in Italy as well.

[179] The general scenario is that a group of buyers incorporates a company which will be their vehicle for the purchase of the target company. The finance will be provided in the form of a bridging loan on the security of a pledge over the shares of the target company and/or of the company newly incorporated to perform the acquisition.

[180] After the merger of the two companies, the bridging finance will be replaced by medium- or long-term financing secured on the assets of the merged company.

[181] Until 2003, the lawfulness of leveraged buyouts was highly debated in Italy, in that said operations were considered as an instrument that a company could use to avoid, through a third party (Newco), the prohibition to subscribe for its own shares (section 2357 of the Italian Civil Code) as well as the prohibition against giving any financial assistance for the purpose of a subscription for or purchase of its own shares (section 2358 of the Italian Civil Code).

[182] Leveraged buyouts were actually given a legitimate status after the 2003 reform of Italian company law, which made it possible to overcome objections to the lawfulness of such operations which had hitherto been raised on the basis of section 2358 (first paragraph) of the Italian Civil Code, which prevents a company from providing either loans or any other form of guarantee for the acquisition of its own shares.

[183] However, according to the 2003 reform, a leveraged buyout is considered the lawful subject to a number of conditions. In particular, pursuant to section 2501*bis* of the Italian Civil Code, the merger plan must indicate how the company's debt resulting from the merger is to be repaid, and the directors of the companies taking part in the operation must prepare an economic and financial plan, to be accompanied by an experts' report endorsing and ratifying such plan, identifying the sources of financing and describing the objectives of the operation.

9 EMPLOYMENT CONSIDERATIONS

[184] Employment relationships are regulated in Italy by the provisions of European regulations and the Italian Constitution, the Italian Civil Code, the National Collective Bargaining Agreements (NCBAs) where applicable, by special laws and regulations (e.g., with regard to working time, part-time) and by individual employment agreements.

[185] The most important Italian labour laws are as follows:

(i) Law No. 300 of 20 May 1970 (also known as the 'Workers' Statute'), which contains 'rules on the protection of the freedom and dignity of employees, of trade union freedom and union activity at the workplace, and on employment in the public sector'.
(ii) Legislative Decree No. 276 of 10 September 2003 (the so-called Legge Biagi), which has reformed the employment market in order to boost employment through the introduction of new types of contracts.
(iii) Law No. 92 of 28 June 2012, which primarily reformed the disciplinary requirements of dismissals.
(iv) The so-called Jobs Act (i.e., the combination of four Legislative Decrees which have been in force since February 2015, but which were recently amended by the so-called Dignity Decree, namely Law Decree No. 87 of 12 July 2018) regarding the social security network, employment services, and active policies, as well as the reorganization of the discipline of labour relations, of inspection activities and of the protection and reconciliation of the demands of care, life, and work.

[186] NCBAs are legally binding only if:

(i) the employer is a member of the labour organization which has signed the NCBA in question;
(ii) the parties (i.e., employer and employee), although not members of a labour organization, agree that such NCBAs are to apply to the employment agreement; or
(iii) the parties implicitly apply such NCBA.

[187] NCBAs are composed of four parts: the 'legal part' (the so-called contenuto normativo), the 'mandatory part' (the so-called contenuto obbligatorio), the management part and the part related to the delegation of particular matters to lower levels of bargaining. The 'legal part' is intended to set out the general terms and conditions of employment, which are to be applied in the various individual employment agreements (such as minimum monthly salary, additional monthly salaries), whilst the 'mandatory part' sets out rights and obligations regarding the relationship between trade unions and entrepreneurs' organizations (such as no-strike clauses, clauses concerning the management of the agreement, disclosure of information, and rights of information).

[188] At a second level, Collective Bargaining Agreements can be negotiated at a company level and at a territorial level and are generally used to integrate the provisions of the NCBAs with regard to specific matters.

[189] The basic definition of employment relationships, as laid down in Articles 2094 et seq of the Italian Civil Code, refers to a subordinate employee as being a worker who has engaged him or herself to co-operate – in exchange for remuneration – in an enterprise by working manually or intellectually under the direction of the entrepreneur.

[190] Under Italian Law, any employment relationship which is not signed on an open-ended and full-time basis is considered exceptional.

[191] Special employment agreements are regulated by the relevant legislation and are permitted either as part of a job-creation scheme or because they are inherent to the nature of the activity performed. The main types of special employment agreements include apprenticeships, part-time contracts, solidarity contracts (which are intended to assist in maintaining employment levels during periods of business difficulty), 'work-training' contracts, fixed-term contracts, job on-call agreements, contracts for the supply of personnel, and agreements with executives.

[192] Fixed-term agreements are regarded as exceptions to open-ended ones. In particular, an employment relationship is always considered an open-ended one, except for those specific cases specified by the Italian law.

[193] Probationary periods can be provided, if the parties so wish, in order to 'allow time to assess the affordability of the employment relationship'. The probationary period clause must be specified in writing; otherwise, the clause will be considered null: moreover, according to Italian case law, such a clause has to be signed at the same time as the employment agreement itself and, in any case, prior to commencement of the employment relationship. During the probationary period, both parties can withdraw from the contract without giving the other the notice period, which is to be applicable post-probation.

9.1 Open-Ended and Fixed-Term Agreements

[194] The termination of the open-ended agreement is a matter for the employee (by resignation) or for the employer (by individual dismissal): the employer's power to dismiss is, however, subject to limits set out by Italian law and by the applicable NCBAs.

[195] According to Italian Law, the maximum duration of a fixed-term employment agreement is twelve months and may be increased to twenty-four months only if at least one of the following conditions is met: i) there are temporary and objective needs, unrelated to the ordinary business; ii) the necessity to replace other employees; iii) requirements connected with significant and non-programmable temporary increases in ordinary activity. In cases of failure to comply with this duration limit, the employer has to pay the employee an indemnity (equal to an amount between two and half and twelve salary months) and the employment relationship will be converted into an open-ended one.

[196] In the absence of specific provisions provided by the applicable NCBAs, the maximum number of employees hired on a fixed-term basis must not exceed 20% of the total number of employees hired on an open-ended basis in force as of 1 January of the year of hire. If the relationship starts during the year, the percentage is calculated on the basis of the number of employees hired on an open-ended basis at the time of the hiring. There are some exceptions to this rule, such as, for example, fixed-term agreements entered into by innovative start-up companies. These are exempted from the numerical limit applied by Italian Law for a maximum period of four years from the establishment of the start-up.

[197] NCBAs can provide for different limits on the number of fixed-term agreements allowed in relation to the total number of employees hired on an open-ended basis. If the maximum number of fixed-term relationships is not complied with, those employment relationships which exceed the limit will not be converted into an open-ended one, but an administrative fine for each fixed-term employee hired in violation of the limit will be imposed, as follows: 20% of the relevant remuneration, for each month or part of a month exceeding fifteen days, if the number of employees hired in violation of the percentage limit is not more than one; 50% of the relevant remuneration, for each month or part of a month exceeding fifteen days, if the number of employees hired in violation of the percentage limit is more than one.

[198] It should be noted that fixed-term relationships cannot be entered into by companies which (i) need to replace employees on strike; (ii) have dismissed redundant employees in the previous six months unless the fixed-term agreement has a duration of three months or is signed in order to replace absent employees; (iii) have suspended employees from service or reduced their working time due to market demand; or (iv) have not performed the risk assessment required by Italian law on health and safety at the workplace. These rules do not apply to those employment relationships for which Italian laws stipulate specific regulations (such as, for instance, those applicable to the start-up phase of a business, or for the period stipulated by the applicable NCBA; or for the purpose of carrying on seasonal activities, or for specific shows and so on).

[199] Executives are expressly excluded from the application of the law concerning fixed-term contracts. A fixed-term employment relationship with an executive can last up to five years. However, the executive can withdraw from the agreement after the first three years, by giving the notice to leave.

[200] A fixed-term agreement can only be terminated at the end of the term provided for by the relevant agreement or for just cause. Apart from the possibility of an employee's dismissal for just cause, the employee can also resign from the employment relationship in case of a just cause (in which case he/she may be entitled to receive compensation for damages equal to the salary to which he/she would have been entitled until the end of the employment relationship unless he/she has in the meantime found a new job). However, if the just cause is found not to exist, the employee, according to Italian jurisprudence, will be asked to pay to the employer a sum by way of compensation for the damages suffered by the employer.

9.2 Disabled Employees

[201] Law No. 68 of 1999 governs the mandatory employment of disabled employees as follows: (i) employers engaging over fifty employees must employ disabled people to the extent of 7% of their workforce; (ii) employers engaging between thirty-six and fifty employees must employ at least two disabled employees; and (iii) employers engaging from fifteen to thirty-five employees must employ at least one disabled employee. Certain categories of employees, other than disabled employees who are already on the payroll (e.g., apprentices, executives) are excluded from the calculation.

[202] This Law No. 68 of 1999 allows a degree of flexibility in selecting the disabled persons to hire, such that employers can hire disabled employees by means of a nominative request (i.e., by indicating to the competent office the name of the particular disabled employee they wish to hire).

9.3 Dismissals

[203] As already pointed out, under Italian law, an employment agreement is always regarded as an open-ended one, except in those cases which are specified by law.

[204] Different provisions apply depending on whether the employee to be dismissed is either a blue-collar or a white-collar worker, or an executive.

9.4 Dismissals of Blue- and White-Collar Workers

[205] Individual dismissals are regulated by the above-mentioned Workers' Statute and the Jobs Act: these provisions refer to blue-collar and white-collar workers, and not to executives. In principle, under Italian law, it is not possible to dismiss blue- and white-collar workers employed on an open-ended basis unless for a just cause or for a justifiable reason (subjective or objective).

[206] According to Article 2119 of the Italian Civil Code, a 'just cause' is represented by a serious violation of the employee's contractual obligations (e.g., stealing, rioting in the plant, damaging plant, materials or machinery by unlawful misconduct, insubordination), such that the continuation of the employment relationship is no longer possible in light of such behaviour. The occurrence of a so-called just cause entitles the employer to terminate the employment agreement without notice of termination or any payment in lieu of notice.

[207] The meaning of 'justifiable reason' is defined by Article 3 of Law No.604 of 1966, which provides for two different types of justifiable reasons: (i) a serious breach of the employee's contractual obligations (the so-called subjective reason, such as lack of productivity or a persistently uncooperative attitude); or (ii) reasons related to productivity, the organization of work and its regular functioning (the so-called objective reason, such as the removal of a work position). The occurrence of a so-called justifiable reason entitles the employer to terminate the employment relationship upon notice of termination (or payment in lieu of notice).

[208] The duration of the notice of termination is defined by the Italian Civil Code as well as by the applicable NCBAs and varies according to the qualification, leve and seniority of the employee to be dismissed.

[209] With regard to the procedure for dismissing blue- and white-collar employ ees, Italian Law provides that the employer is obliged to communicate in writing to the employee to be dismissed both the decision to dismiss him/her and the reason for the dismissal: in case of failure to do that, the dismissal will be considered nul and void. If the employee believes that the dismissal was communicated without a valid and lawful just cause or a justified reason, he/she could challenge the dis missal within 60 days by means of written communication. Then, the employee must file the claim before the court within the following 180 days. Moreover, if the employer – at the time of dismissal – employs more than fifteen employees or – tak ing into account different business units – employs more than fifteen employee (and, in any case, employs more than sixty employees) the procedure referred to above must be preceded (except in limited circumstances) by a conciliation proce dure before the Territorial Labour Inspectorate (the so-called ITL), at the end of which, (and only in the case of a negative outcome), the employer will properly communicate the dismissal to the employee.

[210] With regard to employees engaged prior to 6 March 2015:

(i) If the dismissal is found to be null (e.g., if the dismissal is found to be dis criminatory), whether the employer employs more or less than fifteen employees, he will be obliged to reinstate the employee and to pay him/he a compensation indemnity equal to the last monthly salary from the time of dismissal until the date of reinstatement (which, in any event, could not be less than five months' salary) and to pay the related social security contribu tions. Alternatively, if the employee refuses to be reinstated, the employe must pay him/her an indemnity in lieu of reinstatement equal to fifteen months' salary as well as the compensation indemnity and social securit contributions.

(ii) If the dismissal is found to be void due to the lack of a just cause or a justi fied reason, if the employer employs fifteen employees or less, he will alter natively be obliged to reinstate the employee within three days or to pay him/her a compensation indemnity equal to between two and half months and six months' salary, while if the employer employs more than fifteen employees, he will be obliged to reinstate the employee and to pay him/he a compensation indemnity equal to the last monthly salary from the time of dismissal until the date of reinstatement (which, in any event, could not be more than twelve months' salary) plus the payment of social security contri butions or, if the employee refuses to be reinstated, the employer must pa him/her an indemnity in lieu of reinstatement plus the compensation indemnity and social security contributions referred to above.

(iii) In cases of ineffective dismissal due to the oral communication of the dismissal (instead of in writing), whether the employer employs more or less than fifteen employees, he will be obliged to reinstate the employee and pay to him/her a compensation indemnity equal to the last monthly salary from the time of dismissal until the date of reinstatement (which, in any case, could be less than five months' salary) plus the payment of social security contributions or, if the employee refuses to be reinstated, the employer must pay him/her an indemnity in lieu of reinstatement equal to fifteen months' salary plus the above-mentioned compensation indemnity and social security contributions.

(iv) In case of ineffective dismissal due to the lack of an explanatory statement, if the employer employs fifteen employees or less, he will be obliged to pay compensation to the employee for the damages suffered by him/her while, if the employer engages more than fifteen employees the employment relationship will be considered terminated as from the date of dismissal and the employer will be obliged to pay to the employee a compensation indemnity equal to between six and twelve months' salary.

(v) Finally, if a violation regarding the dismissal procedure occurs, if the employer employs fifteen employees or less he will alternatively be obliged to reinstate the employee within three days or to pay him/her a compensation indemnity equal to between two and half months' and six months' salary, while if the employer engages more than fifteen employees the employment relationship will be considered terminated as from the date of dismissal and the employer will be obliged to pay to the employee a compensation indemnity equal to between six and twelve months' salary.

[211] With regard to employees hired on or after 7 March 2015:

(i) If the dismissal is found to be null (e.g., if the dismissal is found to be discriminatory), whether the employer hires more or less than fifteen employees, he will be obliged to reinstate the employee and to pay him/her a compensation indemnity equal to the last monthly salary from the time of dismissal until the date of reinstatement (which, in any case, could not be less than five months' salary) plus the payment of social security contributions or, if the employee refuses to be reinstated, the employer must pay him/her an indemnity in lieu of reinstatement equal to fifteen months' salary plus the compensation indemnity and social security contributions referred to above.

(ii) If the dismissal is found to be void due to the lack of a just cause or of a justified reason, if the employer employs fifteen employees or less the employment relationship will be deemed to have been terminated as from the date of dismissal and the employer will be obliged to pay to the employee a compensation indemnity equal to between three and six months' salary (based on the last reference salary for the calculation of the severance indemnity) while, if the employer engages more than fifteen employees, he will be obliged (i) in case of obvious absence of a just cause or a justified reason, to reinstate the employee and to pay him/her a compensation indemnity equal to the last monthly salary from the time of dismissal until the date of reinstatement (which, in any event, could not be more than twelve months' salary) plus the payment of social security contributions or, if the employee refuses to be reinstated, the employer must pay him/her an indemnity in lieu of reinstatement plus the above-mentioned compensation indemnity and social security contributions; and (ii) in case of lack of a just cause, justified subjective reason or justified objective reason, the employment relationship will be deemed to have been terminated at the date of dismissal and the employer will be obliged to pay an indemnity equal to between thirty-six months' salary (based on the last reference salary for the calculation of the severance indemnity).

(iii) In case of ineffective dismissal due to the oral communication of the dismissal (instead of in writing), whether the employer employs more or less than fifteen employees, he will be obliged to reinstate the employee and to pay him/her a compensation indemnity equal to the last monthly salary from the time of dismissal until the date of reinstatement (which, in any event, could not be less than five months' salary) plus the payment of social security contributions or, if the employee refuses to be reinstated, the employer must pay him/her an indemnity in lieu of reinstatement equal to fifteen months' salary plus the compensation indemnity and social security contributions referred to above.

(iv) In case of ineffective dismissal due to the lack of an explanatory statement or due to a violation of the dismissal procedure, if the employer employs fifteen employees or less, the employment relationship will be deemed to have been terminated as from the date of dismissal and the employer will be obliged to pay to the employee a compensation indemnity equal to one-half of a month's salary for each year of the employment relationship (in any event, not less than one and not more than six months' salary) while, if the employer engages more than fifteen employees, the employment relationship will be deemed to have been terminated as from the date of dismissal and the employer will be obliged to pay to the employee a compensation indemnity equal to between two and twelve months' salary.

[212] With regard to dismissals effected by employers engaging more than fifteen employees, which have been carried out without the prior mandatory conciliation procedure before the ITL, the employment relationship will be deemed to have been terminated as from the date of dismissal and the employer will be obliged to pay to the employee a compensation indemnity equal to between six and twelve months' salary.

9.5 Dismissals of Executives

[213] As regards executives, the employer can, generally speaking, freely decide to terminate the employment relationship (to the extent explained more fully below) subject to the sole obligation to give notice of termination (except in the event of termination for a just cause). Such a provision is normally included within the

NCBA applicable to the executive. Moreover, the main NCBAs for executives provide that the reasons for the dismissal of an executive must be communicated by the employer to the executive in writing and that, upon termination, the employer must pay to the executive, *inter alia*: (i) any severance pay (the so-called TFR), accrued due to the executive during the employment relationship; (ii) any indemnity due for unused holidays; and (iii) any indemnity due in lieu of notice period. The latter indemnity is due only if the employer decides to terminate the executive's employment forthwith, without allowing him/her to work during the notice period. The amount of the indemnity in lieu of notice depends on the seniority of the executive and can vary from a minimum of six months up to a maximum of twelve months, according to the applicable NCBA. Finally, if the dismissal is found to be unjustified, the executive may be entitled to receive a further indemnity (the so-called Supplementary Compensation) which varies according to the seniority of the executive and his/her age.

[214] Italian Law provides that the dismissal of executives is lawful if based on a 'just cause' or if the dismissal is 'fair' and 'reasonable' (this being a concept different from and less stringent than those of just cause and justifiable reason as provided for the dismissal of blue- and white-collars because the relationship with the executive is stronger – in terms of duties and trust – than that with blue- and white-collar workers). According to the most recent interpretation by Italian jurisprudence, the concept of 'reasonable dismissal' is to be evaluated in accordance with the following criteria: (i) whether or not the dismissal was made on a discriminatory basis; (ii) whether or not the reasons outlined and indicated by the employer in the letter of termination were real and true, as well as consistent with the employer's general needs, (and not simply used as a pretext); and (iii) more generally, whether or not, the employer has behaved towards the executive in good faith and in a fair manner.

9.6 Collective Dismissals

[215] The discipline of the collective dismissal is provided for by Article 24 of Law No. 223/1991 and by Article 8 of Law No. 236/1993.

[216] According to Article 24 of Law No. 223/1991, a collective dismissal takes place upon the occurrence of any of the following: (i) the dismissal concerns a company with more than fifteen employees (by taking into account the number of employees engaged during the previous six months, and not the employees in employment at the commencement of the procedure); (ii) the employer wishes to dismiss at least five employees within the same business unit (or other business units in the same county) within a period of 120 days because of a reduction, transformation or termination of the business activities. However, such dismissal can take place in each productive unit or in more than one, but only if the units in question are located in the same province.

[217] Article 24 of Law No. 223 stipulates that in the event that a collective dismissal takes place, the employer must comply with the provisions set out in Articles 4 and 5 of Law No. 223/1991.

[218] Article 4 provides that an employer who wishes to operate a lawful collective dismissal must comply with a mobility procedure, which would also require consultations with the relevant trade unions. Such a procedure – which can be divided into a 'trade union phase' and an 'administrative' one – is summarized in the next paragraphs.

[219] The employer must give written notice to the trade unions at a company level (the so-called RSA), to the trade union associations or, in their absence, to the most representative trade union associations in Italy, and also to the Provincial Public Office, bearing in mind that any such communication can also be carried out through the employers' associations.

[220] Such written communication must contain the following information: (i) the reasons for the surplus of personnel; (ii) the technical, structural and productive reasons why it is not possible to implement alternative solutions to collective dismissal in order to remedy the situation or to avoid the mobility procedure; (iii) the number, the category and the professional profile of the redundant personnel; (iv) the period of time expected to be required to implement the procedure; (v) the measures, if any, which are expected to be taken in order to deal with the social issues arising from the collective dismissal; and vi) the method of calculating any financial dispensations which are different from those already provided by Italian Law and the applicable NCBA.

[221] The incompleteness of the notice, or the untruthfulness of the information/reasons specified therein, may result in the invalidity of the entire procedure, even if an agreement with the trade unions is reached.

[222] Pursuant to Article 4 of Law No. 223/1991, a copy of the notice must be sent to the Provincial Employment Office.

[223] Within seven days from receipt of the notice, the above-mentioned RSA and the relevant trade association are entitled to request a so-called joint consultation together with the employer, in order to examine the reasons for the surplus of personnel and the possibilities for alternative use of the relevant personnel (for instance, by means of the so-called Solidarity agreement, meaning collective agreements at a company level which provide for a reduction of working time in order to avoid implementing a redundancy procedure). Such a consultation procedure must be completed within forty-five days from receipt of the relevant notice (the term is reduced by half when the number of employees to be dismissed is less than ten). At the end of the consultation procedure, the employer, as well as the trade union organizations which have joined the consultation, will have to notify the competent public office of the outcome of the consultation (also specifying, in the case of a negative outcome, the reason why). The parties could reach an agreement which, in accordance with Italian Law, could provide for the assignment of the redundant employees to different duties or for their temporary secondment elsewhere. On the contrary, if the parties fail to reach an agreement on such a matter, the Provincial Public Office may convene the interested parties in order to carry out a further examination of the issue. Any such procedure has to be completed within thirty days from receipt of the notification of the negative outcome.

[224] Having reached an agreement, or having fulfilled the above-mentioned procedures without reaching an agreement, the employer can proceed to the dismissal and, therefore, must communicate in writing to the employees the termination of their employment relationship, giving them the statutory period of notice or paying them a sum in lieu thereof. At the same time, the employer must communicate in writing to the Regional Public Office, to the Provincial Public Office and to the trade associations: (a) the list of the dismissed employees with their names, places of residence, qualifications, level, age and households; (b) the criteria applied in selecting the dismissed employees (which cannot be provided as a generic list, but has to be explained by reference to each individual employee). Finally, the conclusion of the procedure must also be communicated to the National Social Security Institute (the so-called INPS).

[225] Article 5 of Law No. 223/1991 provides for the criteria to be used in selecting the employees to be dismissed. In the event that the parties have reached an agreement, the criteria to be applied in selecting the employees to be dismissed are those mutually agreed between the employer and the trade unions on the basis of the organizational and production needs of the employer and could be defined in abstract (to the extent that such criteria permit the creation of a ranking system which does not afford any kind of discretion on the part of the employer) or may relate directly to each individual employee to be dismissed.

[226] In general, the following criteria are those to be applied according to Italian Law: (i) households; (ii) seniority; (iii) technical and organizational requirements of the Company. The comparison of each employee's individual position has to be evaluated in accordance with the principles of good faith and correctness and has to take into account the entire organizational and production structure. In any event, it must be noted that an employee may claim the invalidity of the dismissal for either of the following reasons: (i) failure to comply with the written form of the dismissal and with communication and procedural requirements; or (ii) failure to comply with the relevant selection criteria.

[227] In either of the latter cases, the employee must claim the invalidity of the dismissal within sixty days from receipt of the relevant notice of termination.

For employees hired prior to 6 March 2015:

- in cases where there is no dismissal letter in written form, the employer will be obliged to reinstate the employee and to pay him/her a compensation indemnity equal to the last monthly salary from the time of dismissal until the date of reinstatement (which, in any event, could not be less than five months' salary) or, alternatively and upon request of the employee, the employer will be obliged to pay to the employee an indemnity in lieu of reinstatement plus the above-mentioned compensation indemnity;
- in cases of failure to comply with the mandatory communication and consultation procedure, the employment relationship will be deemed to have been terminated from the date of dismissal and the employer will be obliged to pay to the employee a compensation indemnity equal to between twelve and twenty-four months' salary, which will be determined by the judge with regard to the seniority of the relevant employee;

- in cases of violation of the selection criteria, the employer will be obliged t reinstate the employee and to pay him/her a compensation indemnity equa to the last monthly salary from the time of dismissal until the date of rein statement (which, in any event, could not be less than twelve months' salary or, alternatively and at the request of the employee, the employer will b obliged to pay to the employee an indemnity in lieu of reinstatement (equa to fifteen months' salary) plus the above-mentioned compensation indem nity.

For employees hired on or after 7 March 2015:

- in cases where there is no dismissal letter in written form, the employer wil be obliged to reinstate the employee (or, at the request of the employee, t pay the employee the indemnity in lieu of reinstatement) and to pay him/he a compensation indemnity equal to the last monthly salary from the time o dismissal until the date of reinstatement (which, in any event, could not b less than five months' salary);
- in cases of failure to comply with the mandatory communication and consul tation procedure as well as in cases of violation of the selection criteria, th employer will be obliged to pay to the employee a compensation indemnit equal to six and thirty-six months' salary).

[228] The provisions concerning collective dismissal must also be applied t executives, even if subject to the limits and specifications provided by Italian Law In this regard, the mandatory information and communication procedure, the pro visions related to the content of the communications, the mandatory joint consul tation, the examination of the situation before the administrative office, th selection criteria, and the necessity for written form are rules that also have to b applied to executives. Finally, in cases where there is no dismissal letter in writte form and in cases of failure to comply with the mandatory communication and con sultation procedure, as well as in cases of violation of the selection criteria, th employer will be obliged to pay the employee a compensation indemnity equal t between twelve and twenty-four months' salary, without prejudice to the applicabl NCBAs which can provide for different amounts than those provided by law.

9.7 Salary Integration

[229] In cases where a financial crisis suffered by a company leads to the suspen sion or reduction of working time (for a period – whether defined or undefined – c time) for economic reasons, Italian Law allows employers to request the interven tion of a special public fund run by the INPS (the so-called Cassa Integrazion Guadagni), financed from contributions of both employers and employees, whic guarantees to the affected employees a percentage (80%) of the income to whic they would have been entitled during the period of suspension of work or reduc tion of working time.

[230] Intervention by the Fund intervention may be of two kinds: the ordinary intervention (the so-called CIG) and the extraordinary intervention (the so-called CIGS).

[231] The C.I.G. occurs in cases of short-time and transitional financial crisis, not attributable either to the employer or to the employee, when it is foreseeable that the company will resume its ordinary business: in such circumstances, the employer suspends the relevant personnel (or part of the personnel) or reduces the working time. Such a measure applies, amongst others, to industrial companies, certain kinds of craft activities, as well as to certain kinds of cooperative: the beneficiaries of such a measure are all the employees hired on a subordinate basis (including those engaged under an educational apprenticeship agreement, but subject to the exclusion of executives and homeworkers) who have a seniority of at least ninety days. The C.I.G. normally lasts for thirteen consecutive weeks (which can be extended on a quarterly basis to a maximum of fifty-two weeks). It will be possible for companies to access the C.I.G. for 2022 also with reference to the market crisis and the lack of raw materials due to the international crisis situation caused by the Russian-Ukrainian conflict. The C.I.G. intervention is granted, at the request of the employer, by a special commission within the competent office of INPS. Prior to receiving such a concession, the employer must follow the following procedure:

- the employer must communicate to the R.S.A. (or R.S.U.) or, in the absence thereof, to the most representative trade union associations at national level (i) the reasons for the suspension of work or for the reduction of working time; (ii) the foreseeable duration of such a situation; and (iii) the number of affected employees;
- subsequently, each of the parties involved may ask the other for a joint examination of the circumstances of the crisis.

In the meantime, bearing in mind that the above-mentioned procedure must be completed within twenty-five days from the date of communication of the financial crisis (this being reduced to ten days if the employer employs fifty employees or less), the employer must – within fifteen days from implementation of the suspension of work or reduction of working time – submit a request to INPS in order to obtain the concession of the C.I.G. The request must contain (i) the reasons for the suspension of work or for the reduction of working time; (ii) the foreseeable duration of such a situation; (iii) the number of affected employees; (iv) the average number of employees during the previous six months; and (v) the number of hours requested.

[232] The C.I.G.S. can be requested in cases of (i) business restructuring, reorganization or reconversion; (ii) a financial crisis of the company (excluding the company's normal activity shutdowns); or (iii) solidarity agreements (the so-called CDS). It applies to all industrial companies employing more than fifteen employees and to large commercial companies (more than fifty employees); it can be applied to the same employees already defined above with regard to the C.I.G.; its maximum duration varies – without prejudice to the maximum duration provided for the

C.I.G. – according to the basis on which it has been requested (as explained in further detail below); and its intervention is granted, always at the request of the employer, by a Labour Ministerial decree.

[233] Prior to receiving such a concession, the employer must observe the following procedure:

> the employer must communicate – whether directly or through the association of which it is a member – to the R.S.A. (or R.S.U.) or, in the absence thereof, to the most representative trade union associations at national level (i) the reasons for the suspension of work or for the reduction of working time; (ii) the foreseeable duration of such a situation; and (iii) the number of affected employees;
>
> at the request of the employer or of the relevant trade unions (which request has to be filed within three days from receipt of the above-mentioned communication) addressed to the competent office within the region in which the business units are located, or to the Ministry of Labour if the business units in question are located in different regions, a joint examination must be carried out (and must be finished within twenty-five days, or within ten days if the employer hires fifty employees or less) as to the schedule to be followed, the duration of the period of C.I.G.S. intervention, the number of employees involved in the lay-off, any reasons why it is impossible to apply for other kinds of intervention, the measures to be deployed for managing the surplus personnel, as well as the selection criteria to be used for choosing the employees to be suspended, and the application of mandatory criteria for rotation between those employees involved and those not involved in the suspension of work (or the reasons which do not permit recourse to the rotation mechanism).

Then, within seven days from termination of the above-mentioned joint consultation, the employer must file a request in order to be granted the salary integration measure, addressed to INPS, and at the same time to the Ministry of Labour and to the competent Territorial Labour Inspectorate, indicating (i) the average number of employees employed by the employer during the last six months (differentiated by working time), and (ii) the names of the employees affected by the suspension from work or by the reduction of working time. Moreover, the payment of the integration salary is usually anticipated by the employer to the entitled employees at the end of each pay period: such amount will be reimbursed by the INPS within six months after the termination of the ongoing pay period at the end of the concession period.

[234] As already pointed out above, the duration of the C.I.G.S. varies according to the reasons for the suspension from work or for the reduction of working time: twenty-four months in the case of business restructuring, reorganization or revamping, subject to a possible further extension of another twelve, plus a further twelve months; twelve months in the case of a financial crisis of the company. In any event, for both C.I.G. and C.I.G.S., Italian Law provides for a maximum duration limit of thirty months in any period of five years.

[235] The aforesaid Law No. 223/1991 provides that in the case of CIGS, when the company's financial crisis appears to be definitive/terminal, and when the employer is not in a position to re-employ his employees (even if at the moment of termination of the CIGS concession period, the employer has to dismiss only one single employee), he will be obliged to follow the procedure already explained above for the collective dismissal.

[236] In the event that the dismissal is actually implemented, the employer will have to pay to the INPS a contribution equal to 41% of the maximum amount (EUR1 360.77 for 2022) of the monthly unemployment indemnity (the so-called NASPI) for every twelve months of seniority of the employee in the last three years.

[237] However, in the event that the employer is required to pay the contribution for the CIGS (equal to 0.90% of the employee's taxable salary for social security purposes, of which 0.60% is borne by the employer and 0.30% by the employee), the employer will have to pay to the INPS a contribution equal to 82% of the maximum amount of the 'NASPI' for every twelve months of seniority of the employee in the last three years. Finally, in the event of a collective dismissal whose procedure is concluded without reaching an agreement between the parties, the above-mentioned contribution will be tripled.

9.8 Safety Protection at the Workplace

[238] According to Article 2087 of the Italian Civil Code, the employer is obliged to provide the employees with any protective measures which may prove necessary in relation to the specific tasks they perform, to ensure their safety at the workplace. As a result, the employer must adopt all the organizational and procedural measures which are generally taken at any point in time and the safety standards which are normally applied in any given economic sector. Moreover, the Legislative Decree No. 81/2008 (i.e., the so-called Consolidated Act on Health and Safety in the Workplace) provides for a system of precautionary measures that all employers are required to adopt for the purposes of preventing accidents at the workplace and occupational illnesses. Failure to apply those measures would lead to several criminal offences.

[239] The employer is required, in particular, to appoint a person charged with responsibility for evaluating appropriate measures to prevent accidents in the workplace (the so-called RSPP), as well as for arranging a Risk Assessment Document about the possible risks in the workplace (the so-called DVR).

[240] The above Legislative Decree also imposes an obligation on the employer to (i) appoint a so-called competent doctor, meaning a person who is appointed to supervise the medical surveillance of the employees; (ii) provide employees with the necessary and appropriate personal protective equipment; (iii) convene the periodic safety meetings (if the employer employs more than fifteen employees); (iv) consult the Safety Representative of the Employees (i.e., a person who represents the employees and who is appointed directly by the employees or by the trade

unions if the employer employs more than fifteen employees) with regard to the evaluation of risks and to the implementation of the risk prevention measures; and (v) appoint the employees assigned to manage possible emergencies. Another important provision is that in the event that the employer signs a service agreement with a supplier whose activities have to be performed within the employer's premises, the employer must promote and coordinate safety at work by drawing up a single document assessing the risks of interference (the so-called DUVRI), which must be attached to the service agreement and which must indicate the estimated costs of removing such interference (which, if not indicated, leads to the nullity of the service agreement itself).

[241] Finally, the employer is obliged to train: (i) the Safety Representative of the Employees on health and safety matters (if the employer employs more than fifteen employees); (ii) each employee on health and safety matters; (iii) the executives (or people in charge) on health and safety matters.

[242] In case of failure to comply with the above-mentioned provisions, the employer could be sentenced to various criminal sanctions and, in particular, to imprisonment (for a period which would depend on the gravity of the unlawful conduct) or, alternatively, to the payment of a fine (whose amount would also depend on the gravity of the unlawful conduct).

10 INTELLECTUAL PROPERTY

[243] Italy is a party to all the major international agreements on intellectual property, such as the Paris Convention of 1883, the Lisbon Agreement of 1958, the EU Trademark Regulation, 1999 and the Madrid Protocol of 1989.

[244] Italy, as a founding member of the EU, is considered a pioneer in the protection of intellectual property.

10.1 Trademarks

[245] Any person intending to register a trademark may choose between registration in Italy (to obtain an Italian trademark), EU registration (to obtain a Community trademark) and international registration (to obtain an International trademark).

[246] If an Italian trademark is chosen, the application for registration is filed with the Italian Patent and Trademark Office (UIBM) and, with effect from the moment of application, the mark receives protection. The rights arising from the registration of the trademark last up to ten years from the date of submission of the application. The request is examined in terms of legality, non-misleading character and distinctiveness of the mark. If the application is not rejected and there is no opposition by third parties, normally after two to three years, the trademark will be registered.

[247] The Community trademark (*marchio comunitario*) can be requested by filing the relevant application either at the UIBM or at the Office for Harmonization of the Internal Market (OHIM) located in Alicante (Spain). Alternatively, if the trademark has already been registered as an Italian trademark, a petition may be submitted to the OHIM for the extension to Community level of the effectiveness of the registration already obtained in Italian territory.

[248] Once the Community trademark has been obtained, the trademark will have unified and indivisible protection in all of the EU member countries through a single registration procedure (similar to the Italian one), which requires no further formality to be fulfilled in every single national office.

[249] The Community trademark system coexists with national systems of registration of each European country. This means that an earlier national trademark will prevail against a Community trademark and vice versa.

[250] As far as an international trademark is concerned, the application for protection should be based on a prior national registration or a corresponding prior application/registration of a corresponding Community trademark.

[251] This procedure is governed by the Madrid Protocol which has been in force since April 1996 between several countries around the world, including most European countries, the US, Japan, Australia, China, Russia, and, since October 2004, also the EU. The application must indicate the Protocol signatory states in which trademark protection is sought: the protection guaranteed through the international registration of a trademark is equivalent to that provided by a national filing in each of the indicated states. In these states, the effectiveness of the trademark is dependent on the satisfaction of the requirements determined by the law of the relevant state.

[252] The Madrid Protocol provides trademark owners with the opportunity of extending the protection of their trademarks in several countries by simply filing an appropriate application directly at the office of the relevant national or regional authority responsible for trademarks.

10.2 Patents

[253] A tripartite division, similar to the one examined above in relation to trademarks (domestic, European and international), is also applicable to patents. According to Italian law, a patent gives its holder the exclusive right to produce, use and sell a product or a system in the state where the patent application is filed. In particular, if the patent concerns a product, third parties cannot create, use or market that product without the consent of the owner of the patent. If the patent concerns a process/procedure, third parties can neither produce nor market goods produced by using such a process/procedure.

[254] If a person decides to apply for an Italian domestic patent, the application must be filed at the UIBM or at the competent Chamber of Commerce, in order to be assessed for its formal correctness with respect to earlier-patent analysis by the

European Patent Office (EPO). If a positive report is issued, the patent is granted After twelve months from the filing date, the inventor can decide to start the pro cedure for extension of the patent to the European or the international level.

[255] The European patent may be requested by filing the relevant applicatioı either at the UIBM or at the EPO. The applicant must specify in the application th countries for which the protection is requested. It must be noted that the Europeaı patent does not correspond to a single patent on a European scale, but to a 'bundle of national patents, one for each Country indicated in the application.

[256] In case the inventor elects to file for an international patent, he/she/it mus submit their request to the UIBM, the EPO or the World Intellectual Propert Organization located in Geneva (Switzerland), as required by the Patent Coopera tion Treaty (PCT). The application must identify the group of countries (signato ries of the PCT) or 'regions' in which it intends to extend its patent.

11 ANTI-BRIBERY

[257] Normally, Italy does not stand in the highest position in the lists of countrie with the lowest index of corruption. To try to improve this situation, the govern ment has recently introduced certain new provisions aimed at reducing the occur rence of circumstances in which the crime of corruption is easily accomplished.

[258] Law No. 190 of 6 November 2012 has increased the number of situations i which corrupt behaviour, both 'public' and 'private', may qualify as a crimina offence, and subsequently, be punished. This law has also introduced the crime o corruption between private individuals (section 2635 of the Italian Civil Code) an punishes the behaviour of the corruptor (the so-called active crime of private cor ruption) with the same penalties as were previously provided only for the subjec corrupted. The new crime is also introduced in relation to the corruption of publi officials (section 319 of the Criminal Code) and corruption in official records (sec tion 319*ter* of the Criminal Code). In addition to this, the aforesaid law ha increased the list of crimes that, if committed by persons linked to a company apply an administrative liability, pursuant to Legislative Decree No. 231/2001 (*se* the next following section), to the relevant company itself. Legislative Decree No 38/2017 extended the scope of section 2635 and introduced sections 2635*bis* an 2635*ter* of the Italian Civil Code. First, not only the conduct of the private indi vidual who receives money or other benefits, or the promise thereof, but also th conduct of the person who offers money or other benefits, or who promises to per form or omit to perform certain actions, now falls within the definition of crimina conduct. Second, in the event of incitement to bribery by a private individual pur porting to act for the benefit of his company, the latter may also be subject to inter dictory sanctions. These may include the prohibition of the relevant activit suspension or revocation of authorizations, licenses or concessions, the prohibitio against contracting with the public administration, exclusion from facilities, loans grants or subsidies (including revocation of those already granted), as well as th prohibition against advertising goods or services.

12 CRIMINAL LIABILITY OF COMPANIES

[259] Legislative Decree No. 231 of 8 June 2001 has marked a turning point with respect to the general principle of '*societas deliquere non potest*' (i.e., the principle whereby only individuals, and not companies, may be held liable for criminal offences), which characterized the Italian legal system until the enactment of the aforesaid Legislative Decree. This principle had its roots in Article 27 of the Italian Constitution, according to which criminal liability can only be on a personal basis.

[260] The above Decree No. 231/01 provides that where a typical crime is committed and the offender is functionally linked to a company, (whether at the head of the company or in a position 'subject to the direction of others'), and he has taken advantage of or an interest from that company in committing the crime, then in addition to criminal liability of the offender, a personal liability of the entity itself is also engaged for failure to deploy, by way of prevention, measures calculated to prevent and deter commission of the crime. Therefore, there are two different responsibilities, from which are derived two different penalties: one for the offender and the other for the company.

[261] The provision introduces both the general principles and the criteria for the allocation of administrative responsibility and identifies the criminal offences in relation to which the entity's liability arises, together with the requirements for establishing an exemption from such liability, and finally, it describes the penalties for the commission of the crime.

[262] One of the ways for the Company to be exempted from liability, or for its liability to be mitigated, is the implementation of an Organization and Management Plan (modello di organizzazione, gestione e controllo) (hereinafter, the OMP), an instrument introduced by the legislator in Legislative Decree No. 231/01. In the OMP, all areas of the Company's business are analysed with particular attention to those areas in which the commission of a crime is relatively easy, and to all the cautions necessary to avoid the risk of those specified crimes being committed.

[263] The guidelines for the OMP are improving day by day through new, more detailed and specific provisions issued by the Italian legislator. The creation of such OMPs is providing those companies who adopt them with a more solid organization than in the past. Although the OMP is not mandatory, but only optional, it is one of the most appropriate tools provided by the law for obstructing corruption within the business community.

13 INSIDER TRADING

[264] New provisions regarding offences connected with insider trading were introduced by Legislative Decree No. 58 of 24 February 1998, which revoked most of the provisions contained in Law No. 157 of 17 May 1991. The new legislation identifies those persons who are to be regarded as 'insiders': pursuant to section

184 of the above Legislative Decree, insiders are all those persons in possession of privileged information by virtue of their participation in the board of directors, or in the corporate capital of a company, or by virtue of their particular function, whether public, professional or official. In this context, the Legislative Decree defines 'privileged information' as specific information having a specific content which, if disclosed, could materially affect the price of a given security.

[265] Insiders, as defined above, cannot carry out any transactions, even through a third party, in securities in respect of which they have acquired privileged information, nor can they disclose such information to third parties: pursuant to section 184 a penalty involving imprisonment from two up to a maximum of twelve years and a fine from EUR20 000 up to a maximum of EUR3 000 000.00 is provided for. Where guilt is determined a confiscation of securities (as well as of the profits gained via the offence committed) will automatically apply. Furthermore, the above fine may be increased by up to three times or up to the greater amount of ten times the product or profit gained from the crime, in the event that the fine itself is considered to be inadequate in relation to the profits gained or to the personal capacity of the offender.

[266] Section 185 of the Legislative Decree referred to above punishes so-called tipping; anyone disclosing false, exaggerated or tendentious news or creating false transactions or other fictitious devices with a view to distorting the price of securities or creating a false impression of their upward trend may be punished by imprisonment from two up to a maximum of twelve years and by a fine from EUR20 000 up to a maximum of EUR5 000 000.00.

[267] The CONSOB has been granted a specific power and duty to initiate investigation proceedings against all offences provided for by this law. In fact, pursuant to sections 187*octies*, once the public prosecutor has been informed of the offences, he must promptly give notice to the President of the CONSOB.

[268] The CONSOB subsequently carries out the procedure for determining the offences committed, the results of which are reported to the public prosecutor. Furthermore, the CONSOB is granted broad powers of investigation into offences provided for by sections 184 and 185. Pursuant to sections 187*octies*, the CONSOB is allowed, amongst other things, to request information or documents from all persons who may have relevant information about an offence, and is also allowed access to the Tax Register's electronic database.

14 TAXATION

[269] The first considerations in relation to taxation are dependent upon the nature of the parties involved in the transaction.

14.1 Companies

[270] The main income taxes which may be imposed on limited companies are IRES (*Imposta sul Reddito delle Società*, a national tax) and IRAP (*Imposta Regionale sulle Attività Produttive*, a regional tax). Their relevant provisions are to be found in Presidential Decree No. 917 of 1986 (Income Taxes Consolidated Text) for IRES and in Legislative Decree No. 446 of 15 December 1997 for IRAP.

[271] IRES is imposed on the total taxable income of a corporation whose legal or administrative headquarters is situated or whose principal business is carried out within Italian territory. A non-resident entity whose legal or administrative headquarters or principal place of business is outside Italy is subject to Italian tax only on that income which is assessed to have been produced within Italy.

[272] The IRES tax rate is 24% (with effect from the financial year 2017), and after taking into account IRAP – which has a tax rate of 3.9% – the overall tax rate amounts to 31.4%. Taxable profit is determined on the basis of the profit and loss accounts and subsequent fiscal adjustments (which are different for IRES and IRAP).

[273] Capital gains realized by companies are subject to ordinary taxation (IRES and IRAP) and are taxable in the tax period in which they are realized or reported in the books. The gains realized on disposal of depreciable assets may be spread over five fiscal years if the assets in question have been held for at least three years. The gains realized on disposal of long-term investments, provided certain conditions are met, can benefit from the participation exemption regime (i.e., 95% on the gains).

[274] Tax losses incurred in any accounting period by an IRES payer may be carried forward and utilized to offset the profits of subsequent accounting periods without any limitation of time. However, such losses can only be used to offset 80% of the taxable profits of each subsequent period until the losses have been fully utilized (except for newly-incorporated companies, for which there are no limits during the first three years for the carrying forward of losses). Losses do not necessarily have to derive from the same source of income. Losses may never be carried back.

14.2 Individual Income Tax

[275] The taxation of individuals is governed by Imposta sul Reddito delle Persone Fisiche (IRPEF). Taxable income is classified into six categories, each with stated provisions governing its computation and allowable deductions. The six categories are: income from land and buildings, income from capital, income from employment, income from independent work, income from business and income from miscellaneous sources. IRPEF is a graduated, progressive tax with a range of rates from 23% to 43% based on all income derived from any source.

[276] Capital gains arising from the sale of private assets are not generally considered as income. However, the law may, in certain circumstances, assume a speculative purpose. For instance, a capital gain will be classified as income in relation to land or buildings purchased less than five years previously. This figure is then deemed as income for IRPEF purposes and will be subject to taxation accordingly.

[277] For capital gains' in companies that are considered as relevant (more than 25% of voting rights or more than 5% of capital for quoted companies; more than 20% of voting rights or more than 25% of capital for other limited liability companies; more than 20% of capital for remaining companies), there is an ordinary taxation of 49.72% (as of 1 January 2009) on those interests realized. For interests that are not considered as relevant, the substitutive tax on capital gains is applied at a rate of 26%.

14.3 Tax on Real Estate Property

[278] Italian legislation provides for other types of 'indirect' tax (so-called because they do not have as their object income but other types of wealth). Apart from Value Added Tax (VAT), which has no economic effect except on final consumers, the main indirect taxes are:

- Registration tax, which is applied to every transaction which has to be registered. According to the nature of the act, the amount is determined by a fixed charge (generally EUR200) or as a percentage of the value of the transaction (varying from 1% to 15%).
- Stamp duty, which is applied to some written transactions. According to the nature of the act, the amount is determined by a fixed charge or as a percentage of the value of the transaction (generally the cost is not relevant).
- IMU (formerly, ICI), i.e. municipal tax, which is a local house tax charged on the cadastral rent of real estate and land owned.

15 TAX ASPECTS RELATING TO M&A TRANSACTIONS

15.1 Purchase of Shares

[279] Since 1 March 2013, a new tax on the financial transaction (the so-called Tobin Tax) applies on the transfer of ownership rights in shares and similar participating instruments issued by Italian companies, irrespective of the residence of the purchaser or seller and irrespective of the place where the transaction is entered into. The rate of this tax, on a sale of shares of a non-listed company, is equal to 0.2%, and to 0.1% if the transaction is executed on a regulated stock exchange or a multilateral trading facility. As a general rule, the aforesaid tax rates are applied to the consideration paid for the transfer, with specific rules applying in certain cases.

[280] The main tax payable by the sellers is represented by the tax on capital gains (*see* paragraphs [276] and [277] above).

15.2 Purchase of a Going Concern

[281] The deed of transfer of a going concern is subject to the application of registration tax, to be paid within twenty days from the date of the deed. Normally the relevant tax rate is equal to 3% of the current value of the going concern being sold, net of the liabilities resulting from the books or by deeds having a 'certified' date. In relation to specific goods transferred together with the going concern, different tax rates may apply.

15.3 Mergers

[282] As far as mergers are concerned, the tax authorities have traditionally taken the view that they are not part of the ordinary business of a company and, as such, they should not give rise to tax considerations.

[283] As far as corporate tax matters are concerned, the IRES law states, in reviewing mergers and in accordance with the philosophy referred to above, that merger transactions are considered neutral for tax purposes (pursuant to section 172 paragraph 1 of the Presidential Decree No. 917 of 1986 'a merger does not represent the realization or distribution of surplus or deficit of assets of the merged companies').

[284] Indeed revaluation of goodwill covering the difference between the purchase price of the merged companies and the net worth of those companies prior to the merger is not taken into account for fiscal purposes (so it is not possible to amortize the surplus value) and is consequently not taxed. If the company wishes them to be considered for fiscal purposes, it has to pay a substitutive tax (varying from 12% to 16%) on the surplus.

[285] Similarly, the right to carry forward losses for tax purposes of the merged companies by the company arising from the merger is subject to specific limitations. It is possible to use the losses of the merged companies up to an amount not exceeding the net worth of the companies as shown in the merger statement of assets and liabilities, provided that the net worth is quantified without taking into account additions to capital resulting from contributions-in-kind or payments made in the twenty-four months prior to the date of the above-mentioned statement, and provided that the last approved profit and loss account of the merged company shows typical revenue and labour costs exceeding 40% of the average of the previous two years.

[286] In many cases, the government has considered that the above provision have been subject to abuse. An 'anti-evasion regulation' has been introduce whereby fiscal authorities can ignore for tax purposes any tax advantages resultin from a merger carried out without any valid underlying economic purpose, an whose exclusive object was to avoid prohibitions and duties and to obtain undue ta savings.

[287] In the context of a merger transaction, certain additional taxes on busines activities may be imposed. The VAT Decree (Presidential Decree No. 633 of 1972 provides that the conveyance of assets as a result of a merger is not regarded, fo the purpose of the above-mentioned tax, as a transfer of assets, and is, therefore outside the scope of VAT.

[288] Following the principle that VAT and registration taxes are alternative taxe under Presidential Decree No. 131 of 1986 (Consolidated Text of Registratio Tax), mergers are subject to registration tax. In particular, the Decree states tha the filing for registration of corporate documents having as their object, *inter alia* mergers, must be carried out within twenty days.

[289] The registration tax is EUR200.

16 ACCOUNTING TREATMENT

[290] In Italy, the group accounts of certain parent companies, principally liste companies, are required to be prepared under International Financial Reportin Standards (IFRS) as adopted by the EU. Other Italian companies have a choice a to whether they prepare their accounts under Italian GAAP or under IFRS.

[291] IFRS 3 (Business Combinations) and IAS 27 (Consolidation and Separat Financial Statements) are the two relevant IFRS Standards which govern th accounting treatment of business combinations. IFRS 3 was issued in 2004 an updated in 2008. IAS 27 (2008) was issued in 2004 and superseded from 1 Januar 2013 by IAS 27 (2011) concerning Separate Financial Statements, and by IFRS 1 concerning Consolidated Financial Statements.

The method of accounting for business combinations is the 'acquisitio method', which generally requires assets acquired and liabilities assumed to b measured at their fair values at the acquisition date.

It is important to note that under the Italian Civil Code (and as interpreted b the Italian Accounting Organization (OIC)) there are two types of mergers:

(1) All the companies are absorbed and their assets and liabilities are contrib uted to a newly-incorporated company (*fusione propria o pura*). The share holders of the absorbed companies receive shares in the new company i exchange for their shares in the absorbed company.
(2) An existing company absorbs one or more companies (*fusione pe incorporazione/acquisizione*). The shareholders of the absorbed companie receive new shares from the absorbing company.

[292] The Italian GAAP method is the same for both these two types of mergers (OIC 4).

[293] According to the Italian Civil Code:

(i) The consolidation or merger takes effect when the last of the registrations required has been made (i.e., the act of consolidation or merger must, under the responsibility of the notary or of the individuals entrusted with the administration of the company resulting from the consolidation or merger (or of the absorbing company), be filed within thirty days for registration in the office of the register of enterprises. However, in cases of a consolidation or merger by absorption a subsequent date may be established.

(ii) In the first accounts following the consolidation or merger the assets and liabilities are registered at the values resulting from the accounting records at the date on which the consolidation or merger takes effect; if a loss emerges from the consolidation or merger, such loss must be imputed to the individual assets and liabilities of the company participating in the consolidation or merger and, as regards any difference, in compliance with the conditions applicable to goodwill.

(iii) Goodwill may be accounted for as an asset, with the consent of the board of statutory auditors (if any), if acquired for consideration, to the extent of the cost incurred for it, and must be depreciated according to its useful life or otherwise within a period not exceeding ten years.

www.ingramcontent.com/pod-product-compliance
Ingram Content Group UK Ltd.
Pitfield, Milton Keynes, MK11 3LW, UK
UKHW020151290926
15471UKWH00004B/818

9 789403 500867